Prophet AbrahamAbulafia and His Gospel

Spain's Contribution to Understanding the Bible 2

Autumn 2015

Antony Hylton

Contents

Abulafia and the Exegesis of the Prophetic Kabbalah

Introduction

In this book I would first like to identify and locate

Abraham Samuel Abulafia's (1240-1291) place in

Jewish medieval exegesis. To do this I will review the

scholarly literature on Abraham Abulafia and how he

is identified, whether as "rationalist Christian", or

"Anti-Christ" or founder of "Ecstatic Kabbalah" etc. I

would then like to review Abulafia's system of

Exegesis which is developed from the Neo-

Aristotelian exegesis of Maimonides (1135-1204) in

the *Guide to the Perplexed* מורה הנבוכים, the Neo

Platonist exegesis of *Sefer Yetzirah* and the mystical

approaches Eleazar of Worms (Wolfson 2000, p.7)

and Nachmanides n(1194-1270) (Wolfson, 2000, p.

4). Abulafia had a number of teachers divine: the

Angel Raziel (Hames 2007, p.72) and the Angel Yahoel

(Wolfson 2000, p.101) (The Sign Bk. 3) and human:

Rabbi Hillel of Verona (1220-1295) (Hames 2007, 33)

and Rabbi Baruch Togami (Wolfson, 2000 p.111) and

many students, including Prophet Joseph Gikatilla

(1248-1305)[1] (Graetz 1896, 1ff), Rabbi Yehudah

Shlomoh (Wolfson 2000 p.99) and Prophet Nissim

ben Abraham of Avila (Graetz, 1896 p.1ff)[2] (Gottheil,

---

[1] Author of *Gates of Light*

[2] The ministry of Nissim ben Avraham or Avraham of Avila is
mentioned be Responsa 342 of Solomon ben Idret and also
by the testimony of Rabbi Avner of Burgos (Baer, 1961, pp.
280, 330ff) Gottheil states that Prophet Abraham met
Abulafia in Messina. His prophecy regarding the date of
redemption being 1295 instead 1290-91 which was Abulaifa's
date, the sign of the crosses which appeared on the garments
of the Jewish who were clad in the white of yom kippor were
witnessed by Rabbi Avner of Burgos. He called the cross the

1906) and fellow prophetic Kabbalists who may have been influenced by him, i.e Isaac of Acre. He also had a number of enemies, for him these included the Pope Nicholas III (Hames 2007, p71ff) and in reality the foremost Rabbi of Aragon, the successor of Nachmanides Rabbi Shlomoh ben Adret (Rashba 1235-1310).

Abulafia was an avid student under his various tutors and this gave him unique exegetical skills, in his mind suited for the *olam hazeh* and the *olam haba*. If nothing else he can be described as the king of the castle of exegesis or the bridge between Jew and Gentile exegesis or philosophical and peshat or these two together and kabblistic exegesis. I would further like to argue that as a prophet he saw visions

---

seal of Yeshua min Netzeret and turned to Yeshua 25 years later by the appearance of this same sign in his dream.

and dreams and received revelations of *chidut*

(riddles) but that these revelations and prophecies

need to be distinguished from his interpretation of

them and his own teachings, even as Daniel saw

visions and did not understand them so Abulafia saw

visions which he did not fully understand for at least

15 (יה) years (Hames, 2006) (Abulafia, 1943 [1286ff])

and even if he thought he did after 1285 he did not as

evidenced by his new role after 1290 as either a silent

teacher or a dead man[3] (Dan 7-12) or perhaps

following the traditions regarding Moses and Jesus

---

[3] Abulafia disappears in that year Hames calls the disappearance a "vanishing act" (Hames, 2007, p. 53). After that year the year he declared that King Messiah would expose Jesus claim to being son of God and God as lies because Jesus did not operate out of the unified name Yod heh vav heh but only out of yod heh. This of course meant Abulafia and King Messiah were sons of God and "God" because they did operate out of the unified name. Abulafia heard the Acitive Intellect, Yahuah, call him son (Idel, 2012) (Abulafia, [2001]1288).

5

whose bodies both disappear in Jewish tradition[4] [1].

His misunderstanding is seen in his miscalculation

because that which he prophesied and interpreted

using all his seven methods of exegesis did not

happen, indeed both the Roman Church and Jesus of

Nazareth carried on happily in their respective paths

even to this day.

If we were to seek to place Abulafia in a position in

medieval exegesis ranging from conservative to

innovative (Idel, 2007) we will find we can say he is

extremely conservative and extremely innovative. He

is never either/or he is always both/and. For example

the number 363 in his Gematria alludes to the

serpent, the (הנה) who on the *peshat* level is

---

[4] Moses body become a matter of dispute between Michael
the archangel and Satan (Jude 1:9) and the elders of Israel
spread the rumour that the missing body of Jesus was stolen
by his disciples (Matt 28:13)

definitely the evil being. But at the same time it refers to the Messiah (המשיח) the good guy on a *peshat* level. Thus Abulafia absorbs the powers of the serpent[5] and subdues him and uses his power along with the rest of the power available to him as Messiah (Hames, 2007, p. 80). We might say that in Abulafia's mind as Moses was to Israel and Pharoah, so Abulafia was to Israel and Pope Nicholas III. Abulafia using the image of Moses in Exodus as a deliver in the name of Yahuah (yod heh vav heh)[6] interprets Moses as pointing to him as deliver not in 1460 BC[7] but in 1290 AD or at least this is how the

---

[5] (*Teli* in Sefer Yetzira)

[66] This transliteration of the name is line on the research of Sigmund Mowinckel who disagreed with Albright's analysis which lead to the "scholarly guess" of Yahweh (Nachman, 2013) (Hylton, 2013).

[7]

scholars read him today[8].   He drew from the *peshat*

interpretations similar to Rashbam[9] on one extreme

and moving through the *derush*, he loved *Genesis*

Rabbah, of the Amoraic period, he loved the

philosophical exegetes including Ibn Ezra and

Maimonides and he loved the kabbalists like

Nachmanides, and he loved the nations (Franciscans,

Floresians) and though very critical of the

Theosophical Kabbalists because of his sworn enemy

---

[8] However his own words in *Sefer Mafteach Hashmot* gives us
room to doubt their expectation that he planned to be King
Messiah himself because he says "Jesus, however was hung
bodily because he relied upon a material tree, while a
spiritual matter, which is divine intellect, gave the Messiah
eighteen years of life and of these, two years remain" (Idel,
1988/2, p. 52). This statement is the continuation of that
relating to the exposure of Jesus. If as Idel contends Abulafia
is the Messiah in question then this text seems to indicate
that he only has two years to live not that he will defeat
Christianity and bring in the longed for redemption. Idel also
notes that this commentary on Exodus was written in 1289,
18 years after the "revelation in Barcelona" (Idel, 1988/2, p.
52 n33)

[9] And like Rashbam and Rashi and close connection with
Christian contemporaries who he usually called Goyim and
saw the Muslims as Ismael and the Christian s Esau.

(*Rashba*)[10], he respected them more than the philosophers who along with the other Rabbis who rejected kabbalah, were seriously mistaken. But only he and he his disciples had reached perfection of body, imagination, intellect, morals and knowledge required of prophets according to Rambam in the *Moreh,* even mastering as he understood it *yesh"u* and his representative in the *olam hazeh* Pope Nicholas III, and absorbing the power of **Yeshua** **H**anotzri (*Yod Heh* power) into himself as the coming Messiah who would combine *yod heh* with *vav heh* and bring in the age of peace between Jew and Gentile[11] (Hames 2007 p. 87-88) (Hames, 2007, p. 54ff). We will see then Abulafia's place as far as he

---

[10] Although
[11] This vision was in line with the vision of Rambam that all the works of Jesus of Nazareth would turn to the motivation of the nations to serve Yahuah as one in line with the prophecy of Zephaniah read simply.

9

was concerned was the one who would fulfil the hope of Moses (*Sefer Ha Ot*), Maimonides (on prophecy and Messiah and the works of Jesus) (*Hilcot Melakim*) (Nachman, 2012, p. 370)and Nachmanides (the Messiah who would have come only after he went to the pope and said "Let my People Go" (Hames, 2007, p. 71) of the Florensians regarding the coming third age of the Holy Spirit (Hames, 2005). His exegetical methods were designed to restore to mankind the great name of Yahuah and in that name to produce redemption for Israel and the joining of the nations with Israel with one consent (Zeph 3;8ff). We turn now to a review of the literature on Abulafia.

Landauer: Abulafia a Jewish Christian Exegete?

Kaufmann et.al. (1906) hold that Abulafia had a retarding effect on the development of Kabbalah. They also assert that he was "the first one, too, to allow the Christian idea of the Trinity to show a faint glimmer in the Cabala" (Kaufmann & et.al, 1906). In seeking his place among the various medieval exegetes they note:

> He claims to have derived his system of letter-symbols from Moses Nachmanides; but he probably drew it, especially the Gemaṭria and the play with the names of God and the necessary attendant ascetic life and contemplation from the German mysticism of Eleazar of Worms. His view of prophetism or the prophetic gift as the highest goal seems to indicate the influence of Judah ha-Levi's "Cuzari," but his idea of the nature of prophecy itself is rather in accord with Maimonides (Kaufmann & et.al, 1906).

They recognize that Landauer as the "scholar [who] disinterred Abulafia from his long obscurity" He is the earliest and perhaps the most interesting of the critical scholars. Landauer (Landauer, 1845) in a series of studies on Abulafia proposed the hypothesis that

Abulafia was the author of the Zohar (Scholem, 1954, p. 429)[12]. He also refers to Abulafia as a "rationalistic Christian" (Scholem, 1954, p. 379). Bernfeld in his study of Abulafia also came to the same conclusion (Bernfeld, 1931). A sense of Abulafia's special interest in Christianity is also held by Wirszubski (Wirszubski, 1989)[13].

> There is one element in the *Liber Redemptionis* which, unless I am mistaken, is characteristic of Abulafia himself, even if not of prophetic Kabbalah as such. What I have in mind is his interest in Christianity. The author of *Liber Redemptionis* explicitly refers to Christian dogma. In one place he refutes at some length the view that the unity of the knowledge, the knower and the known is identical to Christian dogma of the Trinity. Elsewhere he says that the Christians told him that *shefa'*, that is emanation, is called the Son. (Wirszubski, 1989, p. 90)

Although Scholem, on the hand objects even to the idea that the evidence testifies to Abulafia having "a

---

[12] Unfortunately I was unable to gain access to these studies but their conclusions are generally rejected without going into great detail as to the evidence Landauer used to support his conclusions.
[13] But compare Scholem and (Scholem, 1954) Idel (Idel, 2012)

special inclination to Christian ideas" (Scholem, 1954, p. 129) the ground of his objection are problematic. He points to criticisms Abulafia has of the Trinity but as Scholem himself points out he "acutely criticizes the Kabbalists of his time" (Scholem, 1954, p. 129). This certainly did not disqualify him from having an interest in Theosophical Kabbalah as will be noted by Wolfson (Wolfson, 2000) below, no more than criticizing harshly the accepted Catholic doctrine of the Trinity could remove him from the possibility of being a rationalistic Christian. For this school of thought elements of Abulafia's interpretation of Bible which reminded them of the Zohar lead to him being understood as its author (Scholem, 1954, p. 429).

Scholem points out the kind of elements which may have lead scholars to believe Abulafia was a rationalistic Christian. For example 1. He uses Trinitarian terminology: This is especially in the book ספר מליץ where he uses the terms רוח הקדש and אלוה, גן אלוה for the three aspects of the intellect (Scholem, 1954, p. 380 n.37).[14] 2. "The unintentional similarities of his

---

[14] But Scholem points out some negative aspects of his talk about three in ספר החשק " שלשה שהאלהות אדם לך יאמר ואם

13

"prophetic revelations" with Christian doctrine confused his pupils to such a degree that some accepted baptism" (Scholem, 1971, p. 186). 3. If we add to this the statement of the Florentine prodigy Pico Della Mirandola(1463-1494) "No science can better convince us of the divinity of Jesus Christ than magic and the Kabbalah" and 4. The statement of Idel on Abulafia "It is only in extremely rare cases that we find indications of religious encounters with Christians that were initiated by Jews... Drawn in against their will in these religious discussions, the most Jews could hope for was survival...Nevertheless, during the Middle Ages a major exception to the state of affairs materialized." (Idel, 2012) For Idel this exception was Abulafia. 5. When Yehudah Liebes studied the Christian influences on the Zohar he found at least 9 distinct areas where Christianity probably influenced the Zohar[15] and on completing his study he noted "I

אמור לו שקר וכזב שכן שלשה בגימטריא שק"ר וכז"ב" (Scholem, 1954, p. 380n.37)

[15] In his insightful book *Studies of the Zohar*, Yehuda Liebes observes and gives some specificity to this Christian gospels presence in the Zohar. In this study he shows how in the

suspect that such material is incorporated in the Zohar in many other themes" (Liebes, 1993, p. 160)

---

doctrine of the trinity influenced the three in one conceptions of God in the Shema and the names of Yahuah (Liebes, 1993, p. 140), the concept of the Son (Liebes, 1993, pp. 146-152), the exegesis of Genesis 1.1 (Liebes, 1993, pp. 152-154), the interpretation of the Letter tzaddi as Jesus-Yeshua (Liebes, 1993, pp. 154-158), the idea of the tsaddik descending to hell to "raise up and save the souls of the wicked" (Liebes, 1993, pp. 158-159) (Zohar III 220b), the relationship of love between the disciples of the Zohar reflects the love of the saints for one another (Liebes, 1993, p. 159), the idea of the "limbs of the lady "(Zohar III 231b, II 118a, III, 17a) is seen as a reflection of the Church as a body, all came into the Zohar in a way which allow Christian understanding of the topics into the life of a Jew who would never come across this influence in the synagogue or among his Jewish friends . He also suggests other areas where there may have been an influence for example "the apparent flaw caused to the divinity through Israel's sins, and God suffering in place of mankind, and phrases "reapers of the field" (Zohar III, 127b, Idris Rabba)the name for kabbalists as a translation of the phrase in Luke 10. 1-2. He also notes that a zoharic phrase" the limbs of the Shekinah" is probably related to the Christian conception of the Church as Body of Messiah (Liebes, 1993, p.159). He also suggests that what he calls the central even in the Zohar the assembly of Idra Rabba was not only influenced by the Tannaim but that "the Christian Pentecost may have influenced this theme in the Zohar; this holiday was already of an indubitable mystical character in the New Testament "(Liebes, 1993, p.160) He also sees Christian nuances in certain ideas. He observes the amazing parallels and influences of the Christian teachings upon the Zohar and concludes "The author of the Zohar quite consciously used great quantities of Christian material in his splendid work

15

This was the position held by him and a number of his students until the issue for them finally settled by Scholem (Scholem, 1954). However the fact that having studied the historical circumstances around Abulafia Landuaer could conclude Abulafia was the author of the Zohar says something about the timing of Abulafia and his influence (Landauer, 1845) (Wirszubski, 1989). He was prominent before Moshe De Leone or his contemporaries took on earnestly the task of promoting the Zohar[16] and one of Abulafia's disciples or at least one who is also classified as a prophetic Kabbalist with Abulafia that is Rabbi Isaac of Acre is the only historical testimony we have regarding the early publication of the Zohar. It was he who personally investigated the claims of the deceased Moshe De Leone to have had an ancient book from Shimon Bar Jochai. This all happened after the final fall of Acre in 1291 when the Crusaders were finally expelled from the Holy land. 1291 was also the year that Abulafia had interpreted as the year of redemption, the exposure of the so called false claims of Abulafia's יש"י and the beginning of a new age the *olam haba* where all Israel would be

---

[16] This mainly took place after 1293 (Graetz, 1894)

prophets, for which he wrote many books with the intention of equipping Israel for that age.

Although Landuaer's conclusions have now been rejected by the academic consensus with Idel criticizing him harshly (Idel, 1989) for his misreading of Abulafia in connecting his thinking too strongly with the Speculative position of the Theosophical Kaballah of Moshe De Leone and his disciples, Wolfson (Wolfson, 2000) position holds a position closer to that of Landauer whereby he maintains Abulafia did have an interest in the Sefirotic scheme represented by the Zohar and its literature. The fact that we can have these two varying perspective on Abulafia reflects perhaps more the statement of Jellinek in recognizing Abulafia's "many sided philosophical training". Abulafia claimed to have reached perfect knowledge and this knowledge included every method of exegesis *peshat* and *derush,* Philosophical Allegory, Names Exegesis, and Prophetic exegesis. For Abulafia to have received this level he and his disciples had to be perfect according to the definition of Maimonides and have perfect understanding of Sefirotic Kabbalah. Hence with this view in mind we would expect him to have mastered and exceeded the way of interpreting God and his Word

17

in the Zohar. The idea of Abulafia the rationalist Christian has been left far behind and scholars have taken up a stance of a rigid dichotomy between Abulafia the Jew and Jesus and the Christians. When looking at Jesus for example Hames will add Jesus into Abulafia's "negative" readings even if Jesus is not mentioned: "This implies that the Serpent who misleads Eve, prefigures the false messiah Jesus who is cunning and who will mislead mankind, and because 'he was both cunning and a magician, it [meaning both the serpent and Jesus] was cursed" (Hames, 2007, p. 77) Here Abulafia mentions nothing about a false Messiah, these are Hames words and he uses the term *it*, which clearly refers to one thing but Hames reads it as two things and adds the name Jesus where Abulafia could have but did not have use the acronym יש"ו. It seems that to call Abulafia a rationalist Christian is problematic but the dichotomy drawn between the Jew Abulafia and the non-Jewish Christian into which is lumped the New Testament which of course is a book written by Jews with the sole exception of Luke and at least half to three quarters of it was written to or for Jews is also problematic. This is perhaps shown most clearly by the Hebrew works of Rabbi Avner of Burgos (1270-1348) who according to his Jewish brothers, ex-companions and opponents remains a Jew at heart to his dying day but was writing in Hebrew about Yeshua of Nazareth, the *Moreh Tzedek* (Baer, 1961, p. 330ff) Abulafia may have received most of his knowledge of Jesus from his Catholic and Orthodox contemporaries but he does cite Jesus at least once according to Wolfson: Abulafia quoted "Do not cast your pearls before the swine" (Matthew 7:6), But he does not refer the citation to Jesus but he attributes the citation to the ancients (Wolfson, 2000, p. 92)   Abulafia in *his Sign* sees images reminiscent of the Apocalypse, and like Apocalypse and the NT meditates and reflects on the visions of Daniel and brings forth his own interpretation of aspects of it, as well as using similar terminology.

Jellinek: Abulafia: Exegesis of a False Prophet and False Messiah

In 1853 Jellinek began to publish some of Abulafia's writings. He first published גנזי חכמת הקבלה (Jellinek, 1853), he then published *Philosophie und Kabbala, Erstes Heft, enthaelt Abraham Abulafia's Sendschreiben ueber Philosophie und Kabbala* (Jellinek, 1854) and finally the only surviving *sefer hanevua Sefer Ha*

Oth, Apocalypse des Pseudo-Propheten und Pseudo-Messias Abraham Abulafia, (1887). His perspective of Abulafia is very enlightening. He saw Abulafia as a resurrection of the Essenes. "In the Spaniard Abraham Abulafia of the thirteenth century, Essenism of old found its resurrection. Preaching asceticism and the highest potentiality of the spirit through communion with God, effected by perfect knowledge and use of his names. He was thoroughly convinced of his prophetic mission and considered himself to be the God-sent Messiah. He differs from however from Messiahs who have arisen in different times in his many-sided philosophical training as well as in his perfect unselfishness and sincerity" (Jellinek, 1887) Jellinek published the first printed edition of *The Sign* or *The Letter* under the title *"Sefer ha Oth, Apocalypses des Pseudo-Propheten und Pseudo-Messias Abraham Abulafia"*[17] , the only surviving *sefer hanevuah* of Abulafia. From the title it is clear the view Jellinek held towards the writer of the text

---

[17] (Jellinek, 1887).

"Sefer ha oth" or *The Book of the Sign*[18]*(The Sign)*,
he was both a false prophet and a false Messiah[19].
The genre to which Jellinek assigned the book was
that of an Apocalypse. Jellinek also carried out a
number of other studies on Abulafia. The prophetic
words given in the sign, as distinguished from his
interpretation of them include the following words
spoken on the authority of Yahuah (YHWH) and
extracted from the Sign:

The Word of Yahuah to Abulafia in the Sign

1. Bk1.1 Therefore thus said YHWH, the God of Israel:
2. Have no fear of the enemy,
3. for I and He ([20] הו) will fight against him

---

[18] This is the normal translation of the title but since in Hebrew the word oth applies both to signs and to letters, this bookt could possibly be translated 'The B (Zechariah, 1976)ook of the Letter"

[19] (Hames, 2006)

[20] These two letters represent the second part of the Tetragrammaton which the Melekh Mashiach will come to unite with the first two letters. Abulafia claims that the redemption of Israel by the use of YHWH was prophesied by Moses in his interpretation of Exod 3:14-15. See line 15 and 16 in the Word of YHWH to Abulafia. The transposition letters from vav heh to heh vav does not change their "gematriatic" weight in Abulafia exegetical system.

4. to deliver you from his hand.

5. Let not your heart be weak in the sanctification

6. of the name of the One who wreaks vengeance

7. on behalf of his covenant.

8. Set your hearts, O men, on how to know Yahuah,

9. the God of Israel is his name,

10. and arouse yourselves through him

11. to be wise in his truth.

12. The life of every living being who speaks

13. is He, and he revives the dead

14. and saves the living with the dew of his favor and with generous rain."

15. Who has told from the first to the sons of Israel that they will be redeemed in the name of YHWH?

16. Was it not Moses, the son of Amram, the son of Kehat,

17. the son of Levi, the son of Jacob, the son of Isaac, the son of

18. Abraham, when he recalled in his book the name, "I will be what

19. I will be" and said to them, "I will be has sent me to you" (Ex 3:15).

20. Bk 1.2. Yahuah said to Zechariah, the one proclaiming good news,

21. "Raise your voice with the pen of your tongue[21],
22. and write with three of your fingers the words of this book.
23. God has become a help to his people.

24. Bk 2.1 Then Yahuah said to '|Zechariah[22],
25. "Be well! Go, and I will send
26. you to a nation of a smitten heart, to heal its illness.
27. The balm of my name and my memory (*zechari yah*) I take with you."
28. Bk 2.2 At that time Yahuah said to Zechariah who loves his name
29. ..'Zechariah, my friend, pay attention in my name,
30. for through it you will cleave to me.
31. Please do not reveal its secrets except
32. through his writings'

33. Bk 2.3 Then Yahuah said to me when I saw his explicit and special
34. name in blood my heart was divided between blood for ink[23] and

---

[21] Ps 45:1
[22] The name Zecharyahu occurs at least 18 times in the *Sefer Haot* and is mainly used in the half a book which was written in the year 5045 in the 3rd month by the moon, the tenth year of her cycle in the month of Kislev, which is the ninth month by the sun in the fifth year of it's cycle, on the 6th day which is the first of the month by the count of taken by the years of creation. The name Zechariah does not occur in the last book of the Sign. It's last mention is just before the Book of Melekh ha mashiach

35. ink for blood[24]. Yahuah said to me, "Look, your soul is blood,
36. there, and there is ink, and there is your spirit, and here is
37. your father and your mother, pining for this my name and
38. memorial (Zechari Yah). "

In looking at Abulafia's prophetic exegesis we see that Jellinek is very important in giving attention to his work and in the recognition of the difference between Abulafia and other potential Messiahs. The attention given to the only book of prophecy left among Abulafia's many writings his extremely important. This work represents Abulafia at his peak not just a teacher of Kabbalah or

---

[23] "Just as the ink stand of the scribe is a vessel for the ink that is the matter, so too the number one is a vessel through which every measure is measured. Thus it is said that there are thirteen attributes as the number one, and that is the g"matria for it is one matter" Mafteach hashmot (Wolfson, 2000, p. 139) Here Abulafia says that the13 attributes of Yahuah are measure through Gematria, He has taken the *gimel* and the yod of Hebrew and combined them with the latter word for measure matria.

[24] In the vision Abulafia does a miracle in transforming a poisonous sign on the forehead of Yahuel glorious man. The horseman called it the poison of death and Abulafia called it the elixir of life "for I changed it from death to life" (Sefer Ha Ot Bk III))

expositor of the Torah as seen in his commentaries on the five books of Moses or even his *Imrei hashefer* but a prophet proclaiming *koh amar Yahuah* as can be seen in line 1 above. In this work then we will see the complete Abulafia since Abulafia does not just claim there are seven methods of interpreting the Torah (Abulafia, 1270-1285) but that the as a prophet he uses all seven.

Graetz

Graetz study of Abulafia is interesting because although he recognizes that Abulafia was capable and well educated he also considered that his ideas indicated insanity or that some of his ideas were insane. For Graetz what Abulafia considered a movement toward perfection in speculating on the *Sefirot*[25] and attaining prophecy, Graetz considered this a step backwards from the enlightenment which philosophy had provided through Maimonides and Saadya Gaon. We see in Ibn Ezra a similar attitude which parts company with Abulafia at the point of

---

[25] Mainly the ten Sefirot in the Sefer Yetzirah but he does make correspondents ith the

Gematria[26]. Whereas ibn Ezra would argue that a man should have training in the human sciences before interpreting the Scriptures, he also claimed God did not speak in Gematria. Abulafia would, although influenced by and respecting Ibn Ezra, disagree. He teaches that both the philosophical training was necessary and Gematria was a key to complete knowledge and berates the Rabbis as mistaken who ignore the higher interpretation methods of Gematria, *tzirof* and *natarikon* and *temurah* (Idel, 1988/2, p. 91ff).

For Graetz Abulafia was a disciple of Todros ben Joseph Halevi (1234-1304) of the noble family of

---

[26] " חניכיו - שהנכם פעמים רבות במלחמה ואם לא נזכר. וחשבון
אותיות אליעזר דרך דרש, כי אין הכתוב מדבר בגימטריא, כי יכול
היוכל הרוצה להוציא כל שם לטוב ולרע, רק השם כמשמעו".

"and the count of the letters Eliezer is by way of derash, for the Scriptures does not speak in gematria, for anyone who wishes is able to cast any name for good or for bad. Rather the name is as its simple implication." From

Abulafia (Graetz, 1894, p. 1). Todros was a nephew of Meir Abulafia who was a strong opponent of Maimonides and the rationalistic exegetical approach (ibid. p2). Todros was bitterly opposed to the rational modes of exegesis "He had no words bitter enough against would be wise people who hold everything which appears incompatible with logic as incredible and impossible" (ibid. p2). He may have been initiated into the scret lore by Jacob of Segovia one of the earlier Kabbalists. (ibid. p.2). Graetz sees four major Kabbalists who later spread its exegetical approaches as fruit of the work of Tordros, two dedicated their works to him (ibid p.2). The four Kabbalists were Isaac ibn Latif, Abulafia, Joseph Jikatilla and Moses de Leon. For Graetz Abulafia methods and approaches "obscured the mental light with which men of intellect, from Saadiah to Maimuni, had illumined Judaism, and substituted for a refined religious belief, fantastic and even blasphemous chimeras' (Graetz, 1894, p. 3). Isaac Allatif is said to "stand with one foot on philosophy and with the other on Kabbala"(ibid p.2). He played with philosophical formulae and used mathematical formulae as a key exegetical method "The unfolding and revelation of the Deity in the world of spirits, spheres and bodies, were explained by Isaac Allatif in mathematical formulae" (Graetz, 1894, p. 4). Graetz considers Abulafia as an obscure thinker and a enthusiastic as compared with Isaac. "He endeavored to establish a new order of things by Kabbalistic sophisms" (Graetz, 1894, p. 4) For Graetz Abulafia lead a life of adventure, wrestling for clarity he "fell ever deeper into mazes and illusions"(ibid. p. 4). For Graetz Abulafia saw that the Philosophy path "offered no certainty...to the religious mind thirsting for truth" (ibid. p.4). Indeed what Graetz describes as "trite Kabbala...with its doctrine about Sefiroth, did not satisfy his soul" (ibid. p.5).Abulafia severe criticism of the Speculative system is seen as Graetz as correct. "He, a kabbalist, criticized the unsoundness of this mystic theory so severely and correctly that is it surprising that he should have conceived still more insane notions" (Graetz, 1894, p. 5). Graetz explains that for Abulafia both the philosophical methods and the lower mystical doctrines were but handmaids for his higher system of Kabbala (ibid p.5) (Wolfson,

2000). This resort gaining prophetic insight and divine inspiration for Graetz sets Abulafia apart. 'This means was far from new, but the firm conviction of its effectiveness and his application of it are peculiar to Abulafia" (Graetz, 1894, p. 5). Graetz then outlines clearly the exegetical methods of Abulafia that set him apart from Rambam, Rashbam, Ibn Ezra, Nachmanides and even Moshe Deleon: "To decompose the words of Holy Writ, especially the all hallowed name of God, to use the letters as independent notions (Notaricon), or to transpose the component parts of a word in all possible permutations, so as to form words from them (Tsiruf) or finally to employ the letters as numbers (Gematria), these are the means of securing communion with the spirit world" (Graetz, 1894, p. 5). These are the elements that deal with the higher exegetical methods, Abulafia says Graetz also gave instructions as to life style, where to practice the methods, and what to wear when doing it and even which movements to make and which names of God to recite at which intervals. For Abulafia says Graetz "the plain sense of the words and the simple practice of the religious precepts were merely for the uninitiated, like milk for children. Experts on the other hand, find higher wisdom in the numerical value of the letters and in manifold changes of words" (Graetz, 1894, p. 6). Abulafia did not just practice his paths of exegesis but trained many others. A Samuel, known as a prophet and Joseph Jikatilla (Author of Gates of Light) who both claimed to be prophets and miracle workers(ibid. p.6). He produced prophetic writings in Urbino and moving on a particular of eschatological exegesis used even by Nachmanides whereby as Pharaoh was to Moses and the Hebrew so the Pope Nicholas III was to the Messiah and the Jews[27].

Gershom Scholem(1897-1982)

A statement made by Gershom Scholem in his article on Abraham Ben Samuel Abulafia, transmitter of the kabbalah of the prophets indicates

---

[27] This analogy was used by Nachmanides in his Disputation with Pablo Christiani in 1263.

to some degree some of the results of Abulafia's exegetical *netivoth* at work. Abulafia's exegesis and revelation of the רוח הקדש (Ruach haQodesh-Holy Spirit) and נבוה (*nevuah*- prophecy) and influenced his hermeneutic of *The Letter*. He states regarding Abulafia's revelations "The unintentional similarities of his "prophetic revelations" with Christian doctrine confused his pupils to such a degree that some accepted baptism" (Scholem, 1971, p. 186) This thought is made the more significant when we look at it in the context of his ground breaking lecture on "Abulafia and the Doctrine of Prophetic Kabbalism" included in his seminal work *Major Trends in Jewish Mysticism* (Scholem, 1954) .The importance of the role of Abulafia for Scholem can even be seen in the distribution of chapters in his book. Of the nine lectures only two are given the names of individuals, the first being Abulafia (chap 4) and the second being Isaac Luria. Perhaps as interesting in his lecture is the fact that being Jewish Mysticism there is no chapter on Mysticism of the *notzrim* but if we look at his introduction to prophetic Kabbalah he says there are two sources of authority among all

Kabbalists quoting Isaac ha cohen (1270) "In our generation there are but few, here and there, who received tradition from the ancients...or have been vouchsafe the grace of divine inspiration" (Scholem, 1954, p. 120). Scholem notes the duality is reflected in Kabbalistic literature for hundreds of years and if we compare he statement about what some of them claimed with those of the Apostle whose title for the New Testament believer was *qodeshim* (*hagioi* in Greek) we can see some of the crystal clear parallels. Paul says in Romans 16:25, that his *besorah* was

"according to the *revelation of the mystery*, which was *kept secret* since the world began", and in Colossians 1:26 : (KJV) *Even* the mystery which hath *been hid* from ages and *from generations*, but now is made manifest to his saints:

and Scholem says that even "traditionalists" among the Kabbalists presented innovations "set forth as *interpretations* of the ancients or as *revelations of a mystery* which Providence had seen fit to *conceal from previous generations* [emphasis mine] " (Scholem, 1954, p. 121). Thus for Scholem there is a parallel between interpretations that is exegesis and revelations of mysteries among Kabbalists in general. For Scholem Abulafia is categorized as one who leant "frankly on divine revelation" (Scholem, 1954, p. 120) .

Scholem understood that even after "Kabbalists began to emerge as a distinct mystical group" (Scholem, 1954, p. 119), they were not united. Scholem saw two opposing groups of kabbalists, one represented by those who opposed Maimonides(1135- 1204) and his neo Aristotelian philosophy[28], whose famous names include Moshe De leon[29], and whose representatives desecrated Maimonides grave (Durant, 1950, p. 530),[30] (Baer,

---

[28] Maimonides got his conception of Aristotle from the Muslims and so the Aristotle he dealing with was actually a neo platonic form of Aristotle. (Hofer, 2013)

[29] Moshe De Leon we know was very irritated by the behavior of some of this group who sat around and mocked the words of the Rabbis, and extolled the ideas of the Greeks as explained to us by Doctor Iris Felix in a lecture in 2014.

[30] although with hindsight it is easy to ignore the intensity of this opposition the fact that his supporters could say such things as "From Moses the prophet, till Moses (Maimuni) there has not appeared his equal" (Graetz, 1956, p. 493) and an unknown character left this inscription on his grave "Here lies a man, and still no man, If thou wert a man, angels of heaven Must have overshadowed thy

1961, p. 349)[31]. (Baer, 1961)[32]. These kabbalists are called Speculative or Theosophical Kabbalists[33]

---

mother", but the desecrating kabbalistic opponents replaced the message with "Here lies Moses Maimuni, the excommunicated heretic." This was strong opposition had famous rabbis like Abraham ibn David who some called a prophet vigorously opposed Maimonides. Whereas most attacked and some put Maimonides philosophical writings under the ban Abraham ibn David of Posqueres "subjected Maimuni's Mishne-Torah to scathing criticism, and treated him in a contemptuous manner. He maintained that the author had not thoroughly grasped many Talmudical passages, had misconstrued their sense, and had thus drawn many false conclusions. He reproached him for desiring to bring Talmudical authorities into oblivion by reducing the Talmud to a code, and lastly for smuggling philosophical notions into Judaism" (Graetz, 1956, p. 490) Examples of how disciples of Maimuni brought philosophical concepts into Judaism can be seen in Isaac of Policar's Epistle of Blasphemy as Abner of Borgas calls it. Isaac argued that to know Yahuah in Jeremiah 9:23 meant that man was that "man must know and understand the philosophic theories which explain the existence of God" (Baer, 1961, p. 339). Abner of Burgos retorts the argument is nonsense and points to the meaning from context. Baer notes that Abner of Burgos arguments against the religious rationalists, who were based on the The Guide, were "telling" and "had already been used by the cabalists of the preceding century in their war against rationalism" (Baer, 1961, p. 337)

[31] Among these were also Rabbi Abner of Borgas(1270-1347), Spain, the most famous Jewish convert/apostate from the period who although (Baer, 1961) at one point he moved in rationalist

(Scholem, 1954, p. 124)and it was the fact that they lacked mystical experience and were so speculative

---

circles after his being convinced by a revelation in a dream that the Jesus of Nazareth was the truth, the *Moreh Tzedek* showed that he understood that those who had taken on the pagan philosophy of Aristotle as equivalent to Torah had abandoned their Jewishness, represented by the Bible. "At the end of his *Refutation of the Blasphemer*, Abner charged that Isaac Policar, though he ended his *Epistle* with the signature "a Jew" is not a Jew at all, but a sectarian and a heretic. When it came to the *aggadot* of the Talmud Policar charged Abner with quoting and misinterpreting them, Abner retorted 'You are greatly in error. We do not mean to deny or contradict a thing in the Torah of Moses, God forbid. But we do deny and contradict the interpretation which you and your colleagues put upon the Torah of Moses and we bolster our critique with the words of the great sages who are accepted by you as bearers of your tradition and the ones who received the Torah from the Prophets(cf. Aboth , chap I) (Baer, 1961, p. 348)

[32] In Avner's dispute with Isaac Policar and in his writings he used kabbalah "There can be no doubt that the streams of mystical thought then meandering through Spanish Jewry had a decisive influence upon Abner's thinking in the course of the intellectual crisis" (Baer, 1961, p. 335) Today he would be called a Messianic Jew because even his opponents considered that he didn't fit among the Catholics but was a Jew at heart (Baer, 1961).

[33] This title comes from Gershom Scholem and he calls Abulafia's kabbalah of the prophets 'Ecstatic' kabbalah but we will retain the name Kabbalah of prophecy because Abulafia wasn't looking so much for ecstasy as he was for prophecy.

which lead to Abulafia main criticism of them[34].
Abulafia clearly disagrees with them[35] but does
consider them prophets of a lower level. His work is
built on the foundation of Maimonides *Guide of the
Perplexed* (Moreh). Abulafia wrote a commentary
on the *Moreh* called חיי נפש and סתרי תורה and later
after changing from opponent to kabbalah to teacher
of a kabbalah of prophecy and using in addition to
the *Guide*, *The Sefer Yetzirah*. The prophetic
kabbalah and its main teaching are then developed
from the very teaching which the speculative
Kabbalah of De leon of the Zohar opposed.
Scholem notes the importance of these two streams
represented in their books, "By a curious
coincidence, which is perhaps more than a
coincidence, Abulafia's principal works and the

---

[34] He also accused of having a system of the God head of ten hypostatic sefirot which he considered worse than the Christians who had only three (Scholem, 1954), Abner of Borgas also accused the his fellow Jews of the same thing. Abner converted and in the end around 1281 Abulafia, like Maimonides was excommunicated and had to escape for his life from the from the famous kabbalist Rabbi Solomon ben Abraham ben Adret (Rashba) who called him a charlatan
[35] Rabbi Avner actually asserts that Maimonides changed his mind before he died.

Zohar were written almost simultaneously. It is not exaggeration to say each marks the culminating point in the development of two opposing schools of thought in Spanish Kabbalism" (Scholem, 1954, p. 124). Scholem also notes that "the outstanding representative of ecstatic Kabbalism has also been the least popular of all the great Kabbalists" (Scholem, 1954, pp. 123-124). Indeed Scholem makes the significant point that "Unfortunately, not one of Abulafia's numerous and often voluminous treatise has been published by kabbalists. It waited for Jellinek in the later 1800's for a few of his works to be published (Scholem, 1954, p. 124). It is clear that Abulafia although a kabbalist held to a different kabbalah to that of Moshe Deleon.

According to Scholem, Abulafia had both books of prophecies and Kabbalistic books (Scholem, 1954, p. 124). His prophecies had "unintended similarities" to Christian teaching and led some of Abulafia's disciples taking baptism and joining Yeshua of Nazareth (Scholem, 1971). Idel (Idel,

2012) (Graetz, 1894).[36] He was reputed as a guide to mysticism. Indeed Scholem maintains that as a teacher his teachings were so powerful and could be put into effect by anyone that even though Abulafia "himself never thought of going beyond the pale of Rabbinic Jewry. His teaching can be put into effect by practically everyone who tries" (Scholem, 1954, p. 125). This for Scholem was the reason the Kabbalists refrained from publishing them.

Scholem also made general comparisons between Jewish mysticism and Jewish philosophy. "The mystic, Scholem observes, was wont to view Judaism's concrete manifestations, including the historical fate of the Jews , as symbols pointing to hidden, divine truths, while the philosopher

---

[36] However this is not clear because from the report of Besserman regarding his life it would appear he had problems from the time of his early revelations in Barcelona after 1270 "In his autobiography, Abulafia writes of his dissatisfaction with the first group of students that gathered around him in Barcelona. Accused by Rabbinic critics of teaching Trinitarian doctrines and turning young Jews to Christianity, the thirty one year old Kabbalist again took to the road in search of spiritual guidance- this time inspired by the first of a series of prophetic calls" (Besserman, 2006, p. 120). Although Abulafia had revelations from 1270 he claimed he only wrote sefer nevuoth from 1279.

preferred to interpret them as allegories, reflecting universal truths of reason" (Mendes-Flohr, 1994, p. 4). Whereas the philosopher needs to convert the "concrete realties of Judaism into a bundle of abstractions...By contrast the mystic refrains from destroying the living texture of religious narrative by allegorizing it" (Scholem, 1954, p. 5). For the mystic "the *halakha* was effervescent with symbolic meaning; it was 'transformed [by them] into a sacrament, a mystery rite...Every mitzvah became an event of cosmic importance, an act which had a bearing upon the dynamics of the universe. Through the life of the Torah and mitzvot , the Jews became protagonists in a cosmic drama in which not only the world and Israel are redeemed, but also God Himself" (Mendes-Flohr, 1994, p. 5). Contrary to this says Scholem for the philosopher like Maimonides *halakha* "furnished no material for [their] thoughts" (Scholem, 1954, p. 28). As for Abulafia in particular clearly he was somewhere in between the speculative Kabbalists and the Speculative philosophy. It was Scholem who introduced the term Ecstatic Kabbalah and his chapter on Abulafia in his Major Trends of Jewish

Mysticism brought the knowledge of Abulafia and his system of Kabbalah out of the shadows. His article in the Encyclopedia Judaica in 1971 introduced even more areas which needed investigation.

Scholem's work was important but the introduction of the title Ecstatic Kabbalah causes a focus around Abulafia which was not his main focus. Abulafia was focused on prophecy and being a prophet and with equipping people for the coming age by teaching how to approach Bible so as to be ready. The joy of ecstasy was a side effect but the main focus was reaching the highest level a man could be an *eish milchama*h or a prophet. By introducing the alien term ecstasy although the term prophetic was used alongside it, the focus of academy was sidetracked from the main purpose of the message, to give all men Jews and the nations the chance to enter a messianic age which had as a sign the restoration of prophecy as taught by Eleazar ben Yair, Saadya Gaon and Maimonides. Abulafia distinct hermeneutic was profoundly influenced by his position as prophet and anointed one both terms connected to the role of the Holy Spirit. Jellinek had seen in Abulafia the resurrection of the Essenes and we know that Essenes now known as the *yachad* and special modes of interpreting the prophets for their day called the *peshar*. They were known for their prophetic gifts and also used cryptic writings and *atbash* and other permutation techniques in interpreting Scripture. In the *pesharim* they applied the prophetic words to their teacher and their day. In a similar way the NT read certain scripture as applying to Yahushua and the Church of their day. Abulafia used the numbers, the acronyms and the rewriting of passages of the Tanakh in developing his applicable *peshar*. It was not just a matter of reaching ecstasy but reaching the level of prophecy so as to be able to operate exegetical techniques appropriate in the age of redemption which would begin in 1290/1 and which were needed to reach prophecy.

Moshe Idel

Moshe Idel was not only the successor to Scholem in working with Abulafia and in seeking to elucidate his hermeneutics as prophet but also his greatest critic or corrector (Bloom, 2002). Idel is a prolific writer who wrote many articles in Hebrew and later had them translated. He presented the first results of his research into Abulafia in his mammoth doctoral thesis *Abraham Abulafia* in 1976. There he gives a listing of all the works of Abulafia (Idel, 1976). From 1978 to 1988 he wrote a series of articles on Abulafia based on and expanding his doctoral thesis. From 1988 he began to take selections from his thesis and expand them and published them in a project which envisioned four volumes in which many of the ideas of Abulafia and his writings would be brought to the English speaking academic public through translation of large sections of Abulafia's books with analysis and interpretation of the ideas set alongside the translations. The goal was "to present the major views of Ecstatic Kabbalah" (Idel, 1988, p. Ack.) With his goal being to expose as much of ecstatic Kabbalah to the academic world as possible he used

a method of the translation of large portions of
Abulafia's writings and transliteration of all the
Hebrew titles for the books. This series included
The Mystical Experience in Abraham Abulafia
(Idel, 1988), *Studies in Ecstatic Kabbalah* (Idel,
1988/2), *Language Torah and Hermeneutics* (Idel,
1989). In 2002 he produced a large study. Kabbalah
and Hermeneutics in which he covers many subjects
connected to Abulafia's seven fold exegetical
system, his commentaries on the Guide, his role as
messiah, his commentaries on the Sefirot.

Here the focus was on "Techniques for Attaining
Ecstasy" and the role of music in the "ecstatic
Kabbalah", the Mystical Experience" and "Erotic
Images for the Ecstatic Experience". Thus the focus
was on the ecstasy and the techniques to obtain it
and the experience itself as a mystical experience.
For Idel "Abulafia's system of thought is dominated
by two major concepts: the intellect[37] and the
imagination[38] . The literal meaning of the Torah is

---

[37] (השכל)
[38] (דמיון)

associated with imagination, while its esoteric meaning is associated with intellect" (Idel, 1988, p. 73) For Idel Abulafia's scriptural hermeneutic is characterized by an allegoric approach (ibid. p.73). Abulafia's in his own mind was not just a scriptural interpreter like Rashbam, Rashi, Ibn Ezra and Nachmanides but he understood that as a prophet he was a writer of scripture and sought to have his book prophetic book *Ha-Haftarah* ההפטרה read each shabbat in the synagogue (Idel, 1988, p. 74) (Hames, 2006). For Idel Abulafia's prophetic message flows through the intellect and takes on imagery in the imagination, which means even his visionary imagery as seen for example in *Ha-Ot* contains an intellectual content which can be understood through interpretation (Idel, 1988, p. 74). There are at least two levels to the understanding of the visions, the revealed and the hidden, for two sets of people (Idel, 1988, p. 73). Idel notes that Abulafia sees at least two levels of prophet shown in the fourth of four levels of the "mystical experience" which are preceding by a period of "combining letters" and culminate in a prophet prophesying audibly (Idel, 1988, p. 75).

These four stages to the movement to prophecy are each associated by Abulafia with the Scriptures[39] and thus involve a path of interpretation. The four stages are Stage 1. Apprehension A. The whirlwind (Ez. 1:4, Job 40:6)[40] in this stage you may experience fear and trembling and your hairs on your hair may stand on your head. This is called the "storm of the organs" (Idel, 1988, p. 77) and is followed by an "absence of sensation".[41] Stage 2. Apprehension B. The Spirit or Wind, In *Sitre Torah* this is "another spirit" not the spirit of God. This spirit awakens in the aspiring prophet and gives joy. In *Hayye ha 'Olam he-Ba* היי העולם הבא it is the Spirit of God and connected with the prophecy of Isaiah 11 regarding the branch of Jesse upon whom rests the Spirit of wisdom, understanding

---

[39] And this need to be considered when look at his prophetic exegesis.

[40] This whirlwind is also connected to the blood "moving out" causing trembling and fear which Abulafia connects to Deu 12:23, Lev 17:11. He notes elsewhere that one prophesying will feel like he is about to die. Otzar 'Eden Ganuz (Idel, 1988, p. 75)

[41] Regarding this what we might call being slain in the spirit, we have similar testimony from Abulafia, and anonymous disciple in *Gates of Righteousness* (Idel, 1988, p. 77), R. Judah Albortini

knowledge and the fear of Yahuah[42]. This stage is associated with messianic anointing: and one will imagine that it is as if one's entire body has been anointed with oil from head to feet, and he will be the messiah of God and his messenger" (Abulafia, 1240-1291) (Idel, 1988, p. 76). Thus this stage turns the aspiring prophet into an anointed one and a messenger of Yahuah whose exegesis will clearly take on a level of messianic authority. Stage 3. The tumult which Idel indicates is connected to 1 Kings 19:11-12[43]. This being the case it corresponds to רעש which is usually in BH is translated earthquake[44]. Stage 4. According to Idel this stage

---

[42] This passage in Isaiah 11 is messianic and used in the NT to point to Rabbi Yahushua (Jesus) at his second coming Isaiah 11:4,Matt 3:16, Jn 1:32-33 Rev 5:5, 19:15, 2 Thess. 2:8

1Ki 19:11 ⁴ויאמר צא ועמדת בהר לפני יהוה והנה יהוה עבר ורוח גדולה וחזק מפרק הרים ומשבר סלעים לפני יהוה לא ברוח יהוה ואחר הרוח רעש לא ברעש יהוה:

1Ki 19:12 ואחר הרעש אש לא באש יהוה ואחר האש קול דממה דקה:

[44] Idel indicates that he does not understand the significance of this word but suggests it may be connected to the movement of the limbs mentioned earlier (Idel, 1988)

includes fire which he interprets as visual imagery and speech which Idel interprets as a verbal element. The visual element is a light the early Kabbalists saw which illuminated part of their thoughts. Abulafia calls those that only perceive the light "prophets to themselves" in his letter to R. Judah Salmon (Wolfson, 2000, p. 99). For Abulafia those who reach this level are comparable to the philosophers like Maimonides who know God from his works[45]. For Idel, Abulafia associates prophecy

---

[45] Philosophers are connected to path of interpretation 4 in interpreting the Torah, the early Kabbalists to whom Abulafia refers in the letter are connected to path 5 and possibly move onto 6. But the prophets move along path seven. Drazin (Drazin, 2014) "A Jewish Philosopher first tries to find the truth and then see if the finding is reflected in the Torah. This was Maimonides method. He was impressed with Aristotle's logic and based his thinking on his logic. Then he showed that Aristotelian teaching is in the Torah" (Drazin, 2014, p. 80) According to Saadiah Gaon took a similar approach in his situation. Drazin also goes on to apply Maimonides idea to prophecy "Maimonides, like Rabbi Kook, felt that a prophet is a person with superior intellect who shares his understandings with people. In the Guide 2:34, he states that prophecy comes through an angel. In 2:6 he defines an angel as any force of nature that carries out God's plan, such as wind, rain and the like. The philosopher Gersonides (1288-1344) and others understood Maimonides saying here and elsewhere that prophecy is a natural phenomenon, the use of a higher level of intelligence; prophecy has not ceased"

with those who followed the *Sefirotic* system. He
argues that witnesses for the correctness of this
position are seen in the writings of Isaac the Blind,
R. Azriel of Gerona and R. Ezra of Gerona (Idel,
1988, p. 79)[46]. The second part of this fourth stage
is represented by speech. Abulafia notes that those
who follow the Kabbalah of Names or Prophecy

> ascend from light to light…to the union,
> until their inner speech returns, cleaving to
> the primordial speech which is the source of
> all speech, and they further ascend from
> speech to speech until inner human speech
> [is a] power in itself, and he prepares
> himself to receive divine speech, whether in
> the aspect of the image of speech, whether

(Drazin, 2014, p. 67) . Drazin's point can be modified
significantly on one point, Maimonides drew a distinction
between the reasoning of the nations who considered
prophecy a natural phenomenon and that of the Jews that
was that a man could be perfect in all the ways needed to be
a prophets and still not prophesy because God can choose to
withhold the gift. We see here the philosopher being like the
early kabbalists as prophets to themselves as Abulafia noted
(Idel, 1988, p. 77).

[46] Details of the light experience can be seen in *The Mystical Experience*.

in the aspect of the speech itself; and these are the prophets in truth, in justice and righteousness. (Abulafia, 1887, p. 16) (Idel, 1988, p. 149)

Idel then rereads Abulafia's description in terms of the philosophical terminology Active Intellect who is "God" (Idel, 1988)[47]. In this picture it is clear that when the highest level is reaches Abulafia interprets the experience in terms of the scriptures concepts of truth, justice and righteousness, thus understanding he is living the scriptures, fully.

Idel analyses Abulafia's writings into three main types of books and some miscellaneous writings (Idel, 1988, p. 4). The first type were Handbooks on

---

[47] The image of fire followed by primordial speech followed by intelligible speech are reflected also in the New Testament experience of prophecy. **Act 2:3** And there appeared unto them cloven tongues like as of fire, and it sat upon each of them.
Act 2:4 And they were all filled with the Holy Spirit, and began to speak with other tongues, as the Spirit gave them utterance. These images are also reflected in the Philonic description of what happened as Pentecost at the giving of the Torah and in the tradition of Rabbi Ishmael.

Mystical Experience. These included such books as *Life in the World to Come*, *The Light of the Intellect, Imrei Shefer, Otzar 'Eden Ganuz* and *Sefer ha Heshek*. He also wrote commentaries on Classical Jewish texts including *Sefer ha-Maftehot* a commentary on the Torah and a number of books commenting on *the Guide* of Maimonides and *Sefer Yetzirah*. The third group of books are called *Sefrei ha -Nevuah* and Idel holds with the theory that Abulafia began writing these in 1279 or 5039 (Hames, 2007, p. 72). These books include *Sefer Ha Yashar*, *Sefer Ha-Haftarah* , both of which have been lost, but elements of them can be recovered from commentaries Abulafia wrote on them (Idel, 1988) and *Sefer Ha-Ot* the sole surviving piece of literature of this kind. This is important for us because we are looking at Abulafia the Prophet as exegete not just Abulafia the Rabbi or Wiseman or Philosopher.

The second volume was *Studies in Ecstatic Kabbalah* (Idel, 1988/2). Here he brings together a series of articles covering various aspects of Ecstatic Kabbalah. He observes that Abulafia's "ecstatic Kabbalah was phenomenologically different from the basic mood of the Spanish Kabbalah." (Idel, 1988/2, p. vii). An important observation in regard to Abulafia's place. He according to Idel was claiming to be "prophet and Messiah" (Idel, 1988/2, p. vii). It was this claim which ended up defining his role in relation to the Spanish Jewish community and his place in Jewish medieval exegesis, because it was this claim that lead to him being put under the ban or excommunicated by Rashba (Rabbi J. Adret) and thus him and his exegetical methods as a prophet were 'rejected at the end of the thirteenth century by Spanish Kabbalists' (Idel, 1988/2, p. vii), but then he takes up a position in action and in exegesis in the Italian Jewish community and the Italian monastic communities (Idel, 1988, p. 3) (Hames, 2007, p. 44). Kabbalat nevuah is one of the two names Abulafia gives to his system. The other name is the Kabbalah of names. This approach holds that the Torah consists of a succession names of God. Nachmanides at the beginning of his commentary on the Torah indicated this tradition been lost (Idel, 2002, p. 324). This was of interpreting the Torah was says Idel taken up by Abulafia and his disciples

(Ibid. p.324). Idel also notes that Nachmanides rejected the method of philosophical allegory propounded by Maimonides and others. But Abulafia accepted both the path of name and the path of allegory. In addition Idel notes Abulafia studied one of Ibn Ezra's commentaries on the Torah with Ibn Ezra's Neo-Aristotelian ideas, The Ashkenazi Hasidim and a book called Sefer Shimmush. In noting these varying and sometimes conflicting exegetical method Idel draws attention to an important element in Abulafian exegesis "Only Kabbalistic exegesis, according to Abulafia, can exhaust the plenitude of the text without skipping any of its components and thus in principle take fully into account the textual idiosyncrasies. Abulafia expresses this idea in the strongest terms 'Not one letter is left without being used" during the exegetical enterprise" (Idel, 2002, p. 327)

Idel does not agree with the connection between Abulafia and the eschatological exegesis of the Florensians, the Franciscans and the Cistercians. Nor does he place any significance on the vision Abulafia had in 1276 which Hames considers definitive for Abulafia's activities from 1276 to

1286, which caused Abulafia to believe he was Messiah (Hames, 2005, p. 191) and his revelation in 1286 which left most of his exegesis of the times in place but changed his exegesis of his role in the coming age (Hames, 2005, p. 191). This connection between the date 1290 and the beginning of an age of the Holy Spirit among the Joachimite Franciscan of southern Italy and 1290 and the beginning of the age of prophecy that is of the Holy Spirit is of great importance and Abulafia's justifies the year and the expectation using his three higher exegetical methods of Gematria, Notarikon and Tziruf (Graetz, 1894, p. 5) (Idel, 2002, p. 264) . Whereas the Franciscans justify the years using their exegetical methods based on both the old and the New Testament. Idel also denies the impact of Abulafia's prophetic revelations and exegesis on his disciples which according to Scholem caused some of them to take baptism (Scholem, 1971) (Idel, 2007, 2015.)[48] Idel's focuses too much on the

_____

[48] This is seen in that whereas the Scholem article in the 1971 Encyclopedia Judaica is clear on the fact that Abulafia's revelations were so similar to Christian doctrine that some of

philosophical interpretations of Abulafia experiences and this is problematic because he appears to read Abulafia's prophetic experiences as though Abulafia had control over the experiences and therefore the experiences could be fitted into philosophical boxes of the imagination and active intellect and as though they could then be neatly understood intellectually by Abulafia and others. It is the element of the involuntary elements of the prophetic experience which perhaps need more attention along with that to define a certain aspect of man or God as for example the Active Intellect does not mean the experience of a prophet in the midst of prophecy will confine self to the boundaries of human made definitions. This element of Abulafia perhaps comes out clearest in his experience with Jesus of Nazareth. As explained

---

his disciples took baptism, Idel removes this thought in his 2007 Encyclopedia article. However other scholars hold that this did indeed occur (Besserman, 2006). Perhaps it is connected to the two prophets who appeared in Castile in 1295. Although we have lost Rashba's *responsa* dealing particularly with Abulafia we do have his *responsa* on these two prophets. One called the prophet of Avila who like Abulafia set a date for the beginning

so beautifully by Scholem: "The unintentional similarities of his "prophetic revelations" with Christian doctrine confused his pupils to such a degree that some accepted baptism" (Scholem, 1971, p. 186). Prophecy then if it is truly prophecy can have unintended consequences precisely because the speaker is merely passing on a message from Yahuah or the Active Intellect. The message then, if the prophet is a true prophet is not his but Gods. This aspect needs greater focus in the study of Abulafia and Idel has done.

Wolfson

In his *Abraham Abulafia-Kabbalist and Prophet, Hermeneutics, Theosophy, and Theurgy*, Elliot Wolfson, has focus on the exegesis of Abulafia. He asserts that "Abulafia's kabbalah provides the means for one to attain the spiritual state of the world-to come" (Wolfson, 2000, p. 1) Abulafia for him is a synthesis between Maimonides philosophical ideas, ancient Jewish Esotericism passing through a prism of the German or Ashkenazi pietism a (Wolfson, 2000, p. 2). For Wolfson Abulafia is puzzling and contradictory. His acceptance of the conjunction with Active Intellect (God) and at the same time belief that the philosophical path of cognition was inferior to letter permutations and combinations of the letters of the divine name for achieving the conjunction with the Active Intellect is strange. Wolfson does not however agree with Graetz that Abulafia's ideas were insane (Graetz, 1894). Rather in exegetical terms he sees that Abulafia is forging a synthesis between the positions of Maimonides (philosophical exegesis) and Nachmanides (Kabbalistic exegesis) (Wolfson, 2000, p. 75). The exegetical approach of the path of philosophy and reason cannot according to Nachmanides and Abulafia apprehend the Kabbalah. For Wolfson one key exegetical method used by Abulafia is "the concurrent affirmation of opposites" (Wolfson, 2000, p. 3). This is expressed thus by Wolfson "For, Abulafia the head is the tail, right is left, the merciful one is the judge, the angel is Satan, and so on" (Wolfson, 2000, p. 3).

Wolfson agrees with the position of Scholem that there were two paths of Kabbalah in the 13th century, and holds that Idel extended the historical categories arguing these division remained. He did this to deal with the "relatively monolithic presentation of the history of Kabbalah that has ensued from a neglect of the writings of Abulafia and his disciples" (Wolfson, 2000, p. 3). Whilst Wolfson accepts the criticism he also argues that the typological distinction goes back to Abulafia himself and that he made in his letter to Judah Salomon in order to defend himself against the attacks of Rashba who was a Theosophical Kabbalist (Wolfson, 2000, p. 99). The point Wolfson makes is that not only was the position polemical but that Abulafia often transgressed the bounds of Prophetic Kabbalah and entered into Theosophical Kabbalah. Abulafia's terms for the two Kabbalah's in his *We Zo't li Yehudah* are *qabbalat ha-shemot* and *qabalat ha-sefirot*. Although he criticized the Theosophists, he was influenced theosophic terms and symbols (Wolfson, 2000, p. 5). Wolfson argues Abulafia's system can also be called a Theosophy, *chomat ha-'elohut* as opposed to the divine science of Rambam (Wolfson, 2000, p. 6). For Wolfson then Abulafia's knowledge "embraces both the knowledge of the sefirot and the knowledge of the letters, an idea that traces back to

57

the thirty-two paths of wisdom mentioned in *Sefer Yetsirah*, which consists of ten sefirot and twenty two letters. Both branches of kabbalah are related to the names of God, which are contained in the one unique name, YHWH" (Wolfson, 2000, p. 7). In the Abulafian system both the 10 sefirot and the 22 letters become tools of exegesis. In his system unlike Maimonides the secrets are not there to conceal a potentially problematic theological idea from the masses whilst the intellectual elite are able to comprehend it, but "the secret is a secret because it relates to the divine name" (Wolfson, 2000, p. 4). For Wolfson he see a range of exegetes from conservative to innovative. Abulafia occupies a place between these poles. "As a number of scholars have noted tradition in Judaism embraces the paradox of presenting novel as ancient. What becomes traditional is constructed on the basis of textual expansion by way of creative hermeneutics, which in many way entails the misreading of previous sources" (Wolfson, 2000, p. 5)

Wolfson's studies of Abulafia are very important because they open up wider perspective in understanding the length and the breadth of

Abulafia's learning. That is in understanding the prophetic Kabbalist uses the contextual ways of Rashbam, and Rashi, the philosophical ways of Saadiah Gaon, Maimonides and Ibn Ezra but in addition he uses the mystical interpretations of Nachmanides Moses Deleon and others. He is not like Rashbam focused on a particular approach to the exclusion of others but being "perfect in knowledge" he comprehends what Abulafia calls *sheva netivot* or *shelosh derakim* (contextual, philosophical and kabbalistic) in his exegetic tool box. He understands that as a kabbalist of the higher level the other paths are mastered and excelled in him. Wolfson grasps something very important about Abulafia when he notes the opposites, if the head is the tail and the angel is Satan noting then is simply as it appears. To understand Abulafia requires a stepping back to get the bigger picture, Wolfson reading of the prophets helps us to do that. Wolfson however has not focused on the application of Abulafia's hermeneutics and prophecies to the year of redemption the year 1290-91 nor of his connection with the Franciscans who followed Joachim of Fiore nor with Abulafia's treatment of Jesus whom he only mentions a few times. The next scholar Hames take us further along this path.

Hames: Abulafia *and the Third Age of the Holy Spirit*

Idel notes that it was Y. Baer in his *'Hareka 'Hahistori shelRaya Mehemna (Baer, 1940)* sought to show that the system of Joachim of Fiore influenced certain Kabbalistic writings including *Tikkunei Zohar* (Idel, 1988/2, p. 33). Scholem held that among the 13th century kabbalists there was "an independent Jewish parallel to the doctrine of Joaquim of Fiore concerning the three cosmic stages which correspond with the three figures of the Christian Trinity" which he calls the doctrine of the *shmittahs*. Scholem notes that Fiore's doctrine become popular in the 1240's when it was taken up by the Franciscans (Scholem, 1954, p. 179), at the same time he states that the doctrine of the *shmittahs,* propounded in the work *Temunah,* was codified in Gerona. It was "a mystical interpretation of the twenty two letters of the Hebrew alphabet, and was based on a new interpretation of the Biblical prescription of the Sabbath year, the Shmittah, and the

Jubilee, when all things return to their possessor."
(Scholem, 1954, p. 178).

It is in the studies of Harvey Hames in his in his *Like
Angels on Jacobs Ladder* (Hames, 2007), "From
Calabria cometh the Law , and the Word of the Lord
from Sicily: The Holy Land in the Thought of Joachim of
Fiore and Abraham Abulafia" (Hames, 2005) and his
study "Three in One or One that is Three: On the Dating
of Abraham Abulafia's *Sefer Ha Ot*" that is that we find
a new turn in the studies and the understanding of
Abulafia and his relation to Medieval Jewish Exegesis.
His work on the analysis and dating of ספר האות lead to
a better understanding of that work of prophecy which
has confused so many readers of Abulafia[49]. That work
was a work of Abulafia after he had reached
Maimonidean perfection required of prophets (Bokser,

---

[49] As Dan noted having given a beautiful translation of part of
the prophecy "it is impossible to understand the details of the
apocalyptic vision, which includes elements from the visions
of Daniel and other tradition apocalypses" (Dan, 2002, p.
122). For Dan the books complexity reflects its writer "The
ecstatic and the prophetic, the contemplative and the
messianic, are combined in the tormented soul of this lonely
visionary" (Dan, 2002, p. 122)

1993 [1981], p. 99)[50]. Hames argues that Abulafia's had interactions with the Franciscans who held to the eschatological exegesis based on the writings of Joachim of Fiore. The understanding that a new age of the Holy Spirit would occur in the year 1290-91 or year 5050 on the Jewish calendar. The Francisans, Florensians and Cistercians all understood from their prophetically based biblical exegesis and revelations that a third age of the Holy Spirit would begin during this period. One such group of exegetes were the followers of the visions of Joachim of Flora (Giovanni dei Gioaccini di Fiori) (Durant, 1950, p. 808) among the Franciscans (Hames, 2005) (Lerner, 2001). Joachim had travelled to the Holy Land in the 12th century and had received a vision from God, at Pascha (Easter or resurrection Sunday - Jewish *pesach* season but the

---

[50] "Prophecy is in truth and reality, an emanation sent forth by the Divine Being through the medium of the Active Intellect, in the first instance to man's rational faculty; and then to his imaginative faculty it is the highest degree and greatest perfection man can obtain". (Maimonides, 1135-1204). But the Guide did not satisfy Abulafia desire for prophecy (JE, 1906) (Wolfson, 2000, p. 2).

Christian celebration of the resurrection[51] of Jesus of
Nazareth), which taught him that there would be three
ages in divine history, an age of the Father, an age of
the Son and an age of the Holy Spirit according to its
interpretation of the Scriptures. In *Sefer Haot* (Book 2)
Abulafia describes the priest, Levite and the Israelites as
"ראשי שלשת העו-למים" (Abulafia, [2001]1288, p. 19)
"heads of the three ages". Also Joachim envisaged the
Old and New covenant as two trees. The first tree
planted was Adam running for 63 generations to Christ.
The second tree planted Messiah (AD 30). In this case
42 generations[52] would pass until the beginning of the
final age of the Holy Spirit[53]. In the case of the New

---

[51] In Matthews Gospel Matthew's Jesus describes this event
as an Exodus in his discussions with Moses and Elijah.
[52] Ie the 42 months of 30 days each in the Apocalypse
[53] This came from a reading of the Apocalypse of John chapter
11:2-3 which in turn was a reading of Daniel 7:24-28

Dan 7:24וקרניא עשׂר מנה מלכותה עשׂרה מלכין
יקמון ואחרן יקום אחריהון והוא ישנא מן־קדמיא
ותלתה מלכין יהשפל:
Dan 7:25ומלין לצד עליא ימלל ולקדישי עליונין
יבלא ויסבר להשניה זמנין ודת ויתיהבון בידה
עד־עדן ועדנין ופלג עדן:
Dan 7:26ודינא יתב ושלטנה יהעדון להשמדה
ולהובדה עד־סופא:

63

Covenant each generation would be 30 years[54]. This meant a change was expected in the year 1260 (Lerner, 2001). When this date passed the Franciscans and others who held to Joachim's paradigm fixed on the year 1290 (Hames, 2007). This was 1260 years after the ministry of Christ, that is a time (360years), times (720 years) and half a time (180 years) this equals 1260 years. They expected anti-Christ[55] to be defeated and a new age of the Holy Spirit to begin (Hames, 2005)[56]. This interpretation was built on Joaquim's

---

Dan 7:27ומלכותה ושלטנא ורבותא די מלכות תחות כל־שמיא יהיבת לעם קדישי עליונין מלכותה מלכות עלם וכל שלטניא לה יפלחון וישתמעון: Dan 7:28עד־כה סופא די־מלתא אנה דניאל שגיא רעיוני יבהלנני וזיוי ישתנון עלי ומלתא בלבי נטרת:

[54] Here the 1260 days represented in revelation is read as representing 1260 years and since this period of 1260 days is also represented in the Apocalypse as 42 months this gives 30days a month. The principle of a year for a day is taken from Yahuah's prophecy to Ezekiel in 4:4-6 where he is commanded to bear the sin of Israel and Judah by lying on his side a day for year of sin of Israel and Judah.
[55] Who in the concordant system was parallel to Antiochus Epiphanes persecution of the Jews from 164-167BCE but the new character would be fighting the Church.
[56] This being based on the reading of Dan 7:21-22 and Rev 11:2-3 and Rev 12:6-9

interpretation of John the Revelators interpretation of Daniel 7:25. Daniel speaks of times. John speaks of 1260 days and 42 month of 30 days and Joaquim makes it years based on the year day principle outlines by Yahuah to Ezekiel. Hames relates Abulafia's calculation of this event using different numbers but coming to the same year (Hames, 2007, p. 74). According to Hames (Hames, 2007, p. 40) in 1276 Abulafia on Tevet 5, 5036 (Dec 12 1276) had a revelation which caused him to believe he was the Messiah (Hames, 2007, p. 40)[57]. This vision was the backdrop to much of his Messianic and prophetic exegesis teaching people to prophesy and interpret the scripture prophetically. In this level of exegesis he like the NT writers and the Essenes was writing books he expected Israel to read in their Synagogues alongside the Torah. One such book was called ספר ההפתרה (Abulafia, [2001]1288, pp. 107-134) or הבשור [58] , from this time forth his exegesis and some of his writings would be used to support that date. In 1279 he was in Greece teaching in Patras and Thebes.

---

[57] Cf Idel who does agree with the importance of this vision and so in his outline of Abulafia life his does not mention it (Idel, 1988, p. 3)
[58] (Hames, 2006)

He had a revelation indicating the time was right from him to go on the mission to preach to the pope Nicholas III (Hames, 2007, p. 42). These two revelations of 1276[59] and 1279 are key in helping us understand the complete system of exegesis of Abulafia. But a third stage occurred was reached as Abulafia moved out of the realm of the imagination into the realm of the intellect that is he was granted entrance into the Holy of Holies. He says in one testimony that for 15 years he was with no one to guide and he suffered from satanic visions (Abulafia, 1943 [1286ff]). It was in 1285 or so where he finally enters the holy of holies. This holy of holies for him was the place where the Active Intellect operated. From this position according to Hames, Abulafia prophesied that he would defeat the false Messiah ישו׳ and bring in the new age. In Hames thinking the position was at the top of Jacob's ladder. Hames shows

---

[59] But see below on the dating of this seventh years of Messiah's kingdom, it may be that Hames is overlooking the significance of the revelation in 1270 -71. Rather than measuring the seventh year of Messiah from 1276 and coming to 1283, it is better to calculate the 7th years from 1270-71 when Abulafia first testifies to having had prophetic revelations. This is because in 1288 when he wrote the *Sefer Ha Ot* he dates the vision of *the Sign* in accordance with his first vision claiming he received the revelation of the Sign in the "18th year of his visions".

that Abulafia explained the *Shmittah* leading to the redemption and the place of the beginning of Messiah reign, being Sicily, not Jerusalem and not Israel. To do this Abulafia could take into hand the exegetical methods of prophetic allegory, and the methods of measurement explained in Sefer Yetzirah (Hames, 2005) (Hames, 2007).

Hames reading of Abulafia is enlightening and surely breaks new ground in understanding Abulafia. His studies however suffer from the same problematic Jewish/ Christian dichotomy which the work of Scholem, Idel, and Wolfson suffer from. Ever since Landauer's assertion that Abulafia was a rationalist Christian some scholars have spent a lot of time emphasizing that Abulafia was anti-Christ and that he thought Christianity was a false religion and would disappear in 1290 (Hames, 2007, p. 71ff) (Idel, 1988/2, p. 45ff). One point they tend to emphasize is that for Abulafia *Yesh"u* was "satan" or connected to satan[60].

---

[60] They do not give so much attention to the fact for Abulafia the Active intellect of philosophy became the Metatron of Kabbalah. The Active intellect was Yahuah (YHWH) or the Shekinah inside or with Abulafia and his disciples in the Kabbalistic Holy of holies not in physical Jerusalem but where

For example Hames drums this point home in a declaratory manner: "This is because Judaism was the closest reflection of the Divine revelation and could never be surperseded by anything else, whereas, at best Christianity was a pale image and Total

---

ever they put on tefillin and tallit, dressed in white, as in traditional *yom kippur* clothing took up the tongue, the pen of a ready writer and began their new decreed acts of liturgical worship and entered the holy of holies to use the name as the high priests used to on *yom kippur* when the temple stood (Nachman, 2012). However Wolfson makes the point that in *Mafteach hashmot* Abulafia's key to the book of Exodus there is an interchange of divine attributes of mercy and strict judgment which was especially connected to the process of creation "This interchange is also associated with the dual character of Metatron as a good and evil force, symbolized respectively as the judgmental Satan and the merciful angel" (Wolfson, 2000, p. 172 n213). This process was called *hithappekut hamiddot* or the inversion of attributes "a central theme in his writings that has not yet been discussed in scholarly literature" (Wolfson, 2000, p. 172). In Sefer Hamelitz Abulafia notes that the evil and Samael has an opposite, "the angel" and from this the mequbal can "know that the one which is merciful [the angel] is the judge [Samael] and also the judge is the one who is merciful" (MS Munich BS285 fol. 15a). This points to the mirror principles. The opposite is like an image in the mirror, even as Abulafia understand that is it not Yahuah who spoke to Moses in prophecy, Yahuah spoke to Moses in Moses own voice because philosophically God would need a body and vocal chords to speaks but is incorporal and there when the Torah says God answered Moses by voice, it was Moses voice that was used to communicate to Moses (Wolfson, 2000, p. 73).

misunderstanding of the Torah. Abulafia reading the Torah according to the keys given him by the Active Intellect, was able to incorporate Jesus into the text, and through the use of Gematria, and letter combination and other hermeneutical devices, show the negative aspects of his personality and religious claims" (Hames, 2007, p. 76). Hames goes on to explain that Abulafia was 'extremely negative' to Jesus and Christianity. The problematic element with the approach of Hames here, and that of Idel to some degree, is that they appear to ignore the complexity and apparent contradictions[61] in Abulafia's thought, in addition the rabbinic context into which his words came. For example Abulafia says the "body of Satan... is Tammuz" and Hames comments "While there is no explicit mention here of Jesus, and through the numerical value of all three terms , King Messiah, the body of Satan and Tammuz are the same (453), the latter two are ruled over by the former indicating that

---

[61] Idel does note the perceived contradictions in Abulafia's narrative as read by him but continues his same line of thought without really dealing with the problem of the contradiction, indeed because of his method in translation of transliterating Abulafia's Hebrew letters to English adds, apparent a number of errors of his own (Idel, 1988/2, p. 51)

they are connected with the first half of the tetragrammaton, as is Jesus, and with the sixth day...and it is *plausible* [emphasis mine] to assume that the body of Satan refers to Jesus". Thus we see in this particular case it is not Abulafia who indicates Jesus is the body of Satan but actually this is Hames "plausible" deduction. Jesus is not mentioned. ""Body of Satan" has the same Gematria as King Messiah, but for Hames, through a little deduction the Gematria loses it weight and hence Hames can say Jesus is the "body of satan" although the Gematria of Jesus is 386, 391 or 397 (ישוע,יהושוע,יהושע,). Or if we accept the acronym applied to him by Abulafia and Rabbinic tradition he is 316 יש"ו. Another objection to this negative approach of Hames is that he fails to explain what Wolfson makes clear about Abulafia's exegetical methods as noted earlier: "the angel is Satan", that is Abulafia speaks on many different levels and as with the scales of *Sefer Yetzirah*

> He hath formed, weighed, transmuted, composed, and created with these twenty two letters every living thing , and every soul yet uncreated…These twenty two letters are the foundations, he arranged as a sphere as on a sphere, with two hundred and thirty one modes of entrance. If the sphere

be rotated forward, good is implied, if in retrograde manner evil is intended (Nachman, 2012, p. 192).

Thus the good and the bad are simply based on the direction in which the sphere of the creating alphabet is turned. The failure to understand that Abulafia like Maimonides one of his two main teachers through the *Moreh,* included contradictions and concealed a third or two thirds of his message to keep out the unworthy[62] has led to a complete misreading and underestimation of the role of Jesus, even with the name יש״ו (316) in Abulafia's thought. Regarding the approach of revealing only a third of the exegesis or interpretation and leaving his prophetic disciples to complete the rest of the interpretation that is to complete the exegesis, Abulafia makes a number of

---

[62] We noted above that Abulafia actually cites Jesus with regard to the importance of not throwing your pearls before swine or not telling precious secrets to the unworthy.

important points. He sets them in the context of the

three fold system of exegetes mentioned above:

> The way of tradition (derekh ha kabbalah),
> however is the way that participates with the
> contextual meaning (Peshat) and with wisdom
> (hochmah)[63], and it attests that both are
> true[64]... but in the tradition, there is a
> supplement of ways that are not revealed from
> the contextual sense nor impossible[65] together

---

[63] This is philosophy which means love of wisdom.

[64] This may remind us of the words of Rashbam in outlining
his peshat system, the way of the nonliteral meanings are
true but he will focus on the Peshat. As Kamin notes
"Rashbam presents a very clear distinction between the
literal and the non-literal senses. They differ according to
him, both in content and in exegetical rules by means of
which this content is derived from Scripture. The content of
the non-literal level pertains to law, faith, and moral conduct
(הלכות, הגדות, ודינים). The exegetical rules which govern this,
non-literal use...are the thirteen principles of Rabbi Ishmael-
to be applied to הלכה the legislative sections of the Torah,
and the thirty two principles of R. Eliezer the son of Yose the
Galilean- to be applied to the הגדה.To these two sets of rules
Rashbam adds the typical Rabbinical exegetical consideration,
אריות לשון superfluities or redundancies) (Kamin, 1985, p.
142)

[65] Wisdom of philosophy allegorizes everything that in the
literal reading was to the philosopher impossible or did not
make sense.

with wisdom (Wolfson, 2000, p. 71) (Abulafia,
1271-1290)[66]

He explains further that the way of kabbalah is far

beyond that of contextual and philosophy and even the

intellects of the masters of philosophy cannot bear it

"on account of their ignorance of received truths"

(Wolfson, 2000, p. 71). As a result of this ignorance of

those who followed ordinary Judaism and Philosophy

and the methods of the nations (Catholic and Orthodox

Christians at least) Abulafia,

> the Kabbalist (*he mequbbal*) is not permitted to
> reveal them [the traditions] in his composition.
> Rather he should reveal a measure and conceal
> twice as much (*yegalleh tefach we yakhasseh
> tifhayim*), when he finds a man who is prepared
> and worthy to reveal to him (*peh el peh*) in the

---

[66] There are aspects of the Kabbalah that are never written
down. For examples the esoteric reasons for the
commandments reasons for the commandments for Abulafia
were spoken by God to Moses and then handed down by
word of mouth from Moses to the time of Abulafia (Wolfson,
2000, p. 73)(Imrei shefer) The reasons for them on the peshat
level were explained by Maimonides in the Moreh. For
example in Shomer Mitzvah Abulafia interprets the priestly
blessing, the tefillin and the tallit. In his exposition he explains
"Even though wondrous secrets were revealed from their
sum total , it is not permitted to study their mysteries except
orally, and only after an abundant exertion for the sake of
the truth of the ways of tradition [kabbalah] (Wolfson, 2000,
p. 73)

beginning of his receiving he should reveal to
him two measures and conceal half as much.
(Wolfson, 2000, p. 71) (Abulafia, 1271-1290)

Thus we come to the disturbing point that when we
read Abulafia's exegesis of Jesus we are missing in all
probability two thirds of the message. This missing
element is what may account for the problematic
reading of Abulafia on Jesus found in Hames (2007) and
to some extent in Idel (Idel, 2012).

If we note one of Hames typical negative readings of
Abulafia regarding Jesus this point can be made clearer.
Hames says

Abulafia, reading the Torah according to the
keys given him by the Active Intellect, was able
to incorporate Jesus into the text, and through
the use of gematria, letter combination and
other hermeneutical devices, show the negative
aspects of his personality and religious claims
(Hames, 2007, p. 76)

Let us accept for a moment Hames reading of Abulafia.
For Hames Abulafia did three things with Jesus. (1) He
incorporated him into the text, (2) showed the negative
aspects of his personality, (3) and showed the negative
aspects of his religious claims. Let us take Hames

second point first. He showed the negative aspects of his personality. In basic literary reading of a character we find that personalities are seen by what a person says about himself, what others say about him and what is recorded of his words and deeds. If we now scour Hames description of Abulafia's reading of Jesus, indeed that of Idel ((Idel, 2007) (Idel, 1993) (Idel, 1988/2) and Wolfson (Wolfson, 2000) also we will of course expect to see many citations from the New Testament the only source which contains eye witness and contemporary evidence regarding the personality of Jesus. But we do not find almost a single citation of the gospel nor references to the personality of Jesus and its negative aspects. The man who taught his disciples the Lord's prayer and to love their enemies, "went about doing good and healing all those who were oppressed of the devil" (Acts 2:22). Nor do we find the one who suffered and died for the sins of others and rose from the dead on the third day, we do not find the teacher, the preacher, the prophet or the healer. We do not find even a hint of his Gospel of the Kingdom. His personality is not present accept perhaps in the thought of Hames. We can surely say that the negative parts of the personality of Jesus are not there.

Let us turn now to the incorporation into the text. Here perhaps Hames is on more solid ground. We can look at some of the examples of Jesus incorporation to the text and see that aspect of Abulafia's relationship to Jesus. I would like to preface this with a number of very important points in relation to Hames point that "Abulafia's attitude toward Christianity and its founder is extremely negative" (Hames, 2007, p. 77). First I would like to note the old adage imitation is the highest form of flattery. If this is the case then Abulafia was not extremely negative, but extremely impressed by Jesus for he imitated him in word and deed as we will see below. Secondly If Abulafia is upset with Jesus is it because for him all things in the present age the creation we live in came through the blood in which Jesus was conceived? Thirdly if Hames reading of Abulafia's attitude to Jesus is correct we would be hard pushed to explain how his methods lead to the phenomenon described by Scholem who states regarding Abulafia's prophetic revelations "The unintentional similarities of his "prophetic revelations" with Christian doctrine confused his pupils to such a degree that some accepted baptism" (Scholem, 1971, p. 186). Besseman notes more distinctly:

In his autobiography, Abulafia writes of his dissatisfaction with the first group of disciples that gathered around him in Barcelona. Accused by the rabbinic critics of teaching Trinitarian doctrines and turning young Jews to Christianity, the thirty one year old Kabbalist again took to the road in search of spiritual guidance" (Besserman, 2006, p. 120)

Indeed we can add Hames own words to this list of anomalies if we seek to place Abulafia into the place of an anti-Jesus exegete. Hames notes that Abulafia claims that for יה years he was like a blind man almost going crazy at the revelations he was getting. Both Idel and Hames hold that these dreams and revelations may have included Jesus and Hames notes that Abulafia wrote most of his books in this period when he was like a sheep without a shepherd (Hames, 2006). This places the unintended consequences right back to the beginning of his revelations in 1270 in Barcelona.

Thus a last general point about is that Hames as showed above he reads Jesus into Abulafia's texts because to him what Abulafia says, implies he was referring to Jesus. Hame's way of talking is at times problematic. He does not use terms accurately, for example he talks Abulafia seeing the approaching end of "Christianity"

77

(Hames, 2007, p. 100). He talks of the "falsehood of Christianity and its central dogmas", "the defeat of Teli / Christ and his representative here on earth", which clearly means it is Catholicism he is referring to (Hames, 2007, p. 82). Attention needs to be paid to Abulafia's own terminology when he is dealing with the nations and not the scholars substituted terminology which can misleading. Since Abulafia mentions nations or goyim when talking about the Catholic then scholarship ought to follow him in this, in the same way[67]. Finally we can say that perhaps the key to understanding the role of Abulafia is in the 1/3 of the Kabbalistic tradition which is never written down.

Abulafia was born in the year 1240 when Talmuds were being burnt in France, (Graetz, 1894)

His first book was *get hashmot Divorce of the Names* (1270-71) and his last was either *The Sign* or *Imrei Sefer* (1288). As we have seen above Abulafia has been considered a rationalist Christian (Landauer), a

---

[67] Although Idel notes that in some manuscripts of *Sitrei Torah* Abulafia does refer to Christians as anointed ones and that Jesus called himself anointed one but the Torah calls him a strange god (Idel, 1988/2, p. 54)

resurrection of the Essenes being a unselfish false prophet and false Messiah (Jellinek)[68], an adventurer with following insane notions (Graetz) a founder of Ecstatic Kabbalah (Scholem), A synthesizer of the exegetical conflicting exegetical approaches of Nachmanides (Kabbalah), Eleazar of Worms and Maimonides, (Idel), A prophet who also used the Kabbalah of the Sefirot (Wolfson), A self-proclaimed Messiah, founder of Ecstatic Kabbalah influenced by the teachings and Catholic disciples of Joachim of Fiore (Hames). We can add to these the summary of Abulafia by Joseph Dan on discussing *The Sign* "The ecstatic and the prophetic, the contemplative and the messianic, are combined in the tormented soul of this lonely visionary" (Dan, 2002, p. 122). Is Abulafia a lonely, tormented, ecstatic, prophetic, messianic, contemplative, lonely visionary?

---

[68] The Essenes of the first century were well known for their prophetic gifts and their special interpretation writing. Assuming they are the yachad of the Dead Sea scrolls they also used methods of Tziruf, permutation especially atbash and wrote complete document in cryptic languages. Abulafia's cryptic language in the Sign have cause translators to hop over entire sections of the document and for scholars such as Dan to consider the document "impossible to understand" (Dan, 2002).

Main Idea

In the 7th century AD Islam arose from Arabia. For Greenstein this preceded a new mode of Biblical exegesis called *peshat* (Greenstein, 2005, p. 213) He notes "although the bulk of classical Jewish literature forms an explicit interpretation of the Bible, it is only in the Middle Ages that the genre of the running, direct commentary on the Biblical text into its own as a major phenomenon" (Greenstein, 2005, p. 214) . Preceding this Greenstein maintains was the Midrash or *derash* "The term *derash* derives from the biblical verb *derash*, literally "to seek" but used technically of a divine oracle, primarily of a prophet. The rabbis inquired of the text that which the Israelites inquired of their prophets: revelation" (Greenstein, 2005, p. 216) It is perhaps also true to say that the kabbalah of names (*kabbalat shemot*), the kabbalah of prophecy and the kabbalah of the Sefirot saw a new beginning in 1270/1 AD (5030/31), in Barcelona Spain. Abraham Abulafia is seen by many scholars as the founder of this movement (Hames, 2007) (Scholem, 1954) (Idel, 1988/2). The role of Abulafia in this development was foundational (Scholem, 1971) (Idel, 1988/2). He saw himself as a prophet of the pen, and at the command of the Spirit of the living God or יהוי he wrote and distributed many books and set up schools of prophecy wherever he went and multiplied his books in obedience to instruction of Yahuah (Abulafia, 1943 [1286ff]) (Abulafia, [2001]1288).

Exegetical Ways of the Prophet Abulafia

For Abulafia different exegetical methods reflect the audience and the teachers. Abulafia divides the approach to the Scripture using two numbers, 3 and 7. He calls the three fold division *shalosh derakoth* and the seven fold division *sheva netivot* (Abulafia, 1270-1285). The use of these two numbers is perhaps based on his application of the number systems regarding the alphabet in the *Sefer Yetzirah*[69]. The three paths refer to three kinds of people, the masses, the wise and the kabbalist. The *sheva netivot* are divided between the three. In his letter *The Seven Ways (hanetivoth)* Abulafia outlines the seven exegetical roads to approach the YHWH through the Scriptures, the first three ways for the masses (*hamon*), the middle way is for the philosophers (*balei chochmah*)[70] the upper three ways is for the Kabbalists (*mequbalim*), of these the highest way is spoken prophecy, for him the highest level a man can obtain. For Abulafia the highest way is the same level as Moses who also entered the holy of holies[71]. Another way

---

[69] . His uses of the number three is what allows him to be compared to Christians who teach the Trinity.

[70] This is quite appropriate for Maimonides who considered moderation the chief virtue (Maimonides, 1135-1204, p. ch. 4).

[71] In this Abulafia differs from Maimonides who always set Moses as distinct from the other prophets. Abulafia reaches the highest level in about the year 1285-86 after Y-H yod heh years of wondering around like a blind man, almost driven crazy by the visions he saw, that was because he had no shepherd to teach him. Abulafia does in some places seem to distinguish Moses from the other places but he understood that even as Moses turned water to blood, and Jesus turn

to interpret it is as paths or *netivot* leading up to the Holy of Holies, the place where YHWH the *netivot* are: 1. *peshat* plain or "contextual" (Wolfson, 2000) meaning. 2. *perush*- Interpretative commentary, 3.Derush, Haggadah/Homiletics, and Narrative legend 4.Philosophical allegory 5. Method based on the Book of Creation: Individual letter method[72], 6. Returning letters to their Original State (Restitutio literatum) (Idel, 1989), 7. Names that lead to Prophecy. (Idel, 1989) These *netivot* are paths which lead the user in an ascension in love to Yahuah (*yhwh*). Anyone who masters the seventh method by divine aid[73] has the right to be called יהוה איש מלחמה יהוה שמו, a man of war Yahuah is his name (Ex. 15:3). This title is given to men who reach the prophetic level. Thus in this reading,

---

water to wine, the coming Messiah would turn blood to ink (Sefer Ha OT c.11).

[72] (Idel, 1989, pp. 95-97)

[73] This idea by divine aid may go back to a distinction Maimonides made between the Jewish and the non-Jewish understanding of prophecy. For the non-Jewish philosophers if a man had prepared self for prophecy in being perfect in morals imagination and Intellect he would automatically begin to prophesy, that is see the future etc, but for Israel it was still up to God if he chose to allow a man to prophesy.

Abulafia see Moses as Yahuah a man of war. All of this means the cry to heaven will be answered because through the practices one become part of God's group. In other words once you have reached the highest prophetic level, you will get your prayers answered. Regarding these seven paths Idel notes: "During the period when Spanish Kabbalists began to interpret the Torah in accordance with the fourfold method of interpretation which later became known as PaRDeS in Italy, Abraham Abulafia developed a hermeneutic system based on seven layers of meaning…it is difficult to discern with precision the origin of those method of Exegesis" (Idel, 1989, p. 82) However I would suggest that in light of the central importance of *Sefer Yetzirah* in the Abulafia's system the number three (2 + 1) and seven (6 +1) as a tool of organizing his way of interpreting scripture and nature come directly from there[74]. The first

---

[74] In sefer Yetzirah the alphabet is divided into three groups. The first three aleph, *mem, shin* are called mother. For these shin is seen as hissing like fire, *mem* as cold as water and aleph as balancing between the two. The basis of the three called the balance. In the scale there is one side merit on the

prophetic experience Abulafia claims also goes back to *Sefer Yetzira* (Abulafia, 1943 [1286ff]) Secondly when Abulafia writes to Rabbi Salomon in the late 1280's to defend himself against the damning judgment of Rashba who was a Speculative Kabbalist he gives the typological division of *shenei minim qabbala* (two kinds) of tradition: 1. *qabbalat hashemot* and the 2. *kabbalat hasefirot*.

Regarding the first four ways, Abulafia say "The four paths mentioned... all of the nations (thus the Christians) makes use of them: the masses [make use of] the first three and their sages [make use of] the fourth" (Abulafia, 1270-1285, p. 3) (Idel, 1989, p. 93). As noted by Idel "This observation is indeed noteworthy for this is the first explicit testimony that the fourfold method of Christian exegesis was known to the Jews, and that comparison between the Jewish and Christian hermeneutic methods, according to the kabbalist, bears out the

---

other criminality and the balancing between them the tongue.

similarity."[75] The first level is to help man who is "born a wild ass" to move closer to Yahuah through "traditions until he becomes an exemplar of the accepted faith" (Idel, 1988/2, p. 83) This level was for people who had just learned to read or were taught Torah by others(ibid p.83). The goal is to educate the masses to good deeds by fear as in the curses in Deuteronomy 28:12. The fear was provoked so the people could watch God do battle for Israel (ibid. p. 85) (Abulafia, pre 1285, p. 171a). They need not fear since "it is their Master and your Master who is doing battle on your behalf" (Abulafia, pre 1285, p. 171a) (Idel, 1988/2, p. 85).[76] "They [the enemy] will die an unnatural death before your eyes, you will behold and your hearts will be glad"(ibid)[77]. The second way applies to

---

[75] This observation supports the hypothesis of Bacher and Scholem that the Kabbalists developed their methods of exegesis from the Christians (Idel, 1989, p. 93)

[76] This battle between their master and your master will appear in *The Sign*.

[77] Abulafia wrote about the death of his enemies in The Sign after he saw Pope Nicholas, die the very night before he was aiming to present himself to him, from the first chapter of the Sign verse dalet it seems he feels he had personally killed the pope by stabbing the pope with the spear of his tongue which

parts of the Scriptures which cannot be obeyed or explained in a literal manner for example the circumcision of the heart cannot be physical and the oral tradition explains it as repentance(ibid 87) however the circumcision of the child "must be taken literally" (Abulafia, 1270-1285, p. 2) (Idel, 1988/2, p. 87)[78].

The third way in relation to *derush* is exemplified in when a Sage explains unexplained elements in the Biblical text for example: "Why on the second day of creation God did not say "it is good?" In this relation Idel says h*aggada* refers to rendering the scripture attractive to draw the heart towards Yahuah. In The *Treasures of the Garden of Eden* Abulafia gives an example of this way. "the word *'sh* [man] refers to [the angel] Gabriel, as it is

---

was the name Yahuah, He "killed his [Yahuah's] enemies with righteous judgement", it seems that Abulafia believes he killed more than one person and the pope represented Pharoah, and Abulafia must then be Moses.

[78] Abulafia also goes into mystical explanations of circumcision in the higher interpretation methods (Wolfson, 2000, p. 87). He also interprets circumcision in line with Sefer Yetzirah

written "Gabriel the man ['sh]… alternatively we may say that 'sh refers to Adam, as it is written "to this one we shall give the name 'shah [woman] for this one was taken from man['sh] …we may say 'sh refers to Moses, or, that it refers to Messiah, as it is written "Behold a man ['sh] Zemah is his name and from beneath him shall sprout…" and so to "God is his name," for in the future time when the Messiah will come he will be called [by the name of] God. This is the name the Righteous Lord will bestow on him. To conclude, [we may say] there is no end to the matters of Derush." (Idel, 1988/2, p. 90).[79] The fourth way is also very important. The followers of this way were taught an esoteric meaning which approached the understanding of the philosophers such as Aristotle and Plato. The students of this way "removed from most of the Torah from [the level of] plain meaning, and were quite aware of this. And they tread the path of philosophy and said that the entire Torah [consists of] parables and enigmas"

---

[79] Interestingly Abulafia placed the commentaries of Rashi, son of Ibn Ezra and Nachmanides into this way of interpreting the Tanakh.

(Abulafia, pre 1285, p. fol 9a)[80]. Abulafia illustrates this way with Exodus 15:3 "The fourth method is based on the procedure of philosophy wherein the power of intellect is denoted by [the name of] God, and they would state that he is constantly at war with the limbs of the body. The higher powers of the soul of the soul are called 'the children of Israel' and the corporal powers are referred to as 'the Egyptians'." (Idel, 1988/2, p. 92) (Abulafia, pre 1285, p. 171b).[81] How radical an

---

[80] that this method was associated with the Qehilah (Church) can be seen from a citation of R. Joseph Bekhor Shor, who when commenting on Number 12:8 notes "from here is broken the arms of the of the nations of the world, who say that everything Moses said was 'allegoria' i.e. enigma and parable, and not what the plain meaning purports to say." (Idel, 1988/2, p. 191 n.46). Ibn Ezra confirms this but with a little more accuracy "And **one [emphasise mine]** of the methods of the uncircumcised sages who say that the entire Torah consists [merely] of enigmas and parables" (Friedlander, 1877, p. 1) (emphasis mine) Idel points out that Ibn Ezra did not approve of the way but Abulafia made use of it because Maimonides used it in his *Guide*.

[81] This idea of the intellect warring against the limbs of the body can clarify some of the more obscure passages in *The Sign*, and in terms of the NT we can begin to see that the Intellect in Abulafia in like the Spirit in Paul. The corporal powers are called "flesh" in Paul. So he says For the flesh wants what is contrary to the Spirit and the Spirit what is

understanding this position can be seen in Abulafia's comments on Adam, Eve and the Serpent. He argues that if their story is taken at face value "the story would be laughable. And it is clearly not the intent of the Torah to relate laughing matters"[82] (Idel, 1988/2, p. 93). The philosopher investigates the inner meaning (*penimiyuto*), says Abulafia when his intellect cannot bear the plain meaning.

The ways 5, 6, and 7 what Idel calls Abulafia's Kabbalistic Hermeneutic. The first the way of *Sefer Yetzirah*[83] has a focus on individual letters (Idel, 1988/2). It is here that the appearance of large letters (Gen 1:1, Deu 6;4) and small letters(Gen 2:4), inverted letters (Num 10: 35-36) are interpreted. Also included here are the understanding of *qetib-qere*, and the omission or

---

contrary to the flesh. They are at war with one another". Gal 5:17.

[82] We have testimonies of Moshe De leon reflect on the attitude of the philosopher types and how they would in private be laughing at the words of the Rabbis. Abulafia gives us some sense of the material they would consider amusing.

[83] He uses this title in *'Otzar 'Eden Ganuz*

inclusion of *vavs* and *yods* in spelling. Abulafia notes that "This fifth [method] is the first of the levels of interpretation reserved only for Kabbalistic sages of Israel, and it constitutes a method different from that used by the masses. It is also different from the methods used by sages of the nations of the world[84], and differs from the methods used by the Rabbinic sages of the Israel who make use of the [first] three methods (Idel, 1988/2, pp. 96-97). Indeed in this case he says "those who tread the path of the nations[85] will mock this method...Yet they are gravely mistaken" (Idel, 1988/2, p. 97) Here Abulafia classifies the Rabbinic sages of Israel with "the sages of the nations of the world". Thus his position in relation to the Exegesis of the Jews and that of the nations is similar, he perceives himself as above them both. We will see this in this argument regarding the use of Adonai in stated of

---

[84] Notice he does not use the term Christianity, for he speaks as the Rabbinic sages talk.
[85] Here he clearly refers to the Jewish philosophers with whom he used to associate. He too like the used to be against the Kabbalah as his teacher Rabbi Hillel of Verona was.

Yahuah (YHWH) and the use of the Father Son and the Holy Spirit instead of Yahuah.

The sixth way is what Idel calls *Restituti Literatum* but Abulfia calls it *Zeruf Otiyot*- Letter Combinations. Abulafia describes it as "returning all the letters to their prime-material state and you i.e., [the practitioner] give them form in accordance with [your] insight" (Idel M. Ibid, 97). Hereunder Abulafia included *notarikon, gematria, tzeruf* or permutation. For example the acronym *yesh"u* (Rabbinic notarikon for Jesus*)* bore the gematria 316. In terms of *Sefer Yetzirah* this was its weight. Other words and phrases with the same number in the creative acts of Yahuah at the beginning carried the same weight. In the Book of Creation (S. Yetzirah) letters are building blocks of the creation of all things and the number values they are given represent the weight they had. The weight 316 is carried both by the new name given to Yeshua by the Rabbinic lore, and carries the same weight as אלהי בכר *elohei nekar*[86] and by this Rabbis would

---

[86] Josh 24:20, Jer. 5:19

allude to Jesus. Abulafia cites *Yetzirah* regarding this method "Twenty-two cardinal letters; He engraved them and hewed them and weighed them and permuted them and combined them and formed by their means the souls of all formed beings and [the souls] of all that in the future will be given form."(Idel, Ibid, 97). Thus Y-Sh-U-A ישוע (salvation) could be read as שועי Sh-U-A-Y (highest), This according Abulafia is its primary weight, which Idel reads as "equivalent letter and numerical value". This is its own primary weight. The established scaled include words with the same value so for Yeshua (386) that might include *lashon* לשון, tongue or tzeruf צירוף, combination.[87] Then the letters can be considered individually, as in י ש ו ע yod shin vav ayin, and combine them in different ways. Here Abulafia also includes *atbash*[88] and other substitutionary methods. Thus Yeshua in

---

[87] These two words are very important one's for Abulafia's language system (Idel, 1989, 8-9)

[88] This method of substituting aleph for tav and bet for sheen and *gimel* for resh was used by the Essenes and may have been used by the translators of the LXX in Jeremiah 51 where Jeremiah calls Babel, Shishak, which when transformed using atbash give BBL.

atbash might produce מבפז M-B-P-Z which can
mean priceless or it can be recombined to produce
במזם (*brings to*). He would also take for example the
last letters of the words of a verse and make a new
word or the first letters of a verse. He also adds a
multiplication technique for example יה Yah (15)
times יה Yah (15) is 225 and וה VH times והVH is
121, together giving 346. "The one who practices
the sixth method is likened to the Active Intellect,
who gives form to matter"(Idel, 1989, 101).

The final method that way of names that leads to
prophecy is called holy of holies and gives "the
inner sense of the inner meaning" (Idel 1989, 101).
Abulafia appears to claim to have reached this
method in the years 1286 after 15 years of torment
by jealous spirits: "From the year 1281-1285 the
Lord was with me to deliver me from all troubles.
At the beginning of the year 1285 the Lord brought
me into the Holy Temple and that was the time
when I completed this book which I wrote here at
Messina for my precious, honorable, wise and
understanding pupil" (Abulafia, 1943 [1286ff], p.
23). This *netivah* includes all the other methods
(ibid 105). The goal is prophecy by the

transformation of the verse of the Torah to names of God. For this Abulafia illustrates with Exodus 15:3 Yahuah יהוה איש מלחמה יהוה שמו. In this method all these words are read as one word eg

יהוהאישמלחמהיהוהשמו. We can consider each letter as a word. This does not involve the transposition of letters. "It is as if you yourself create the words and their conventional meaning"(Idel 1989, 103).This was a method clearly used by Nachmanides who applied it to Genesis 1:1

בראשית ברא אלהים את השמים ואת הארץ. Nachmanides made the point that the original Torah did have the division of the words we see today and reread the text:

בראש יתברא אלהים. In the head He created himself Elohim. Abulafia sees this method as the crown of all the methods. He calls this method the seal within the seal and when this way is accomplished "then you can immediately succeed in all that you endeavor and God will be with you"(ibid, 102). In this method he refers to the 72 letter name of God, "72 names, from 22 letters, which are 22 names of each and every letter of the Torah" and he notes "You create the words and confer onto them [or innovate] a [new] meaning."(Idel 1989, 103). Here again emphasizes that the practitioner decides on the meaning in accordance with your wish. He uses the verb create (*bara'* ברא) for the practitioner a verb which is only used of God in the Tanakh. In regard to this method Abulafia sees the Messiah as creating a new world. Idel parallels his thought with a midrash which states "In the future the Holy One, blessed be He, will reveal His Explicit name to each and everyone of the righteous in the world to come. By its means are created a new heaven and a new earth"(Midrash *Otiyyot de Rabbi Akiva'*)(Idel 1989, 104) This midrash acts as a guiding light for Abulafia. His whole purpose was to teach the *Shem Meforash*.

Now that we have seen the main methods of Abulafia and can see clearly that he was not like Rashbam who focused on one main method and honored the other Rabbis who were focused on other types of exegesis, rather Abulafia was the opposite, he used all the methods. But he did not just interpret for Jews but also he felt having been rejected by his brethren, the Holy Spirit commanded him to preach to the Gentiles, and when he did, they believed him (Abulafia, [2001]1288). He had one problem however the Gentiles to whom he was sent already had a Messiah whose name was Yeshua min Netzeret. We will now look at how Abulafia related to these problems.

As noted above many scholars understand Abulafia had a special problem with Jesus and Christianity and less so with the Judaism of the Rabbis of his day. Abulafia as the King Messiah Zecharyahu, however had the main task of restoring the name Yahuah to Israel and to the nations. This was his overriding concern. Every one Jesus, Judah and the nations had to submit to his revelation of the unifying and use of the Tetragram. Thus he had with the Rabbis the problem of the refusal to use Yahuah and the custom of substituting *Adonai* which went back to the second temple period (Nachman, 2012) (Nachman, 2013). Also he had to deal with the Christians and the problem of calling God, the Father, Son and Holy Ghost. Both of these terms were used instead of Yahuah (YHWH). After dealing with the issue of the name of God he had to deal with the name and person of the Messiah. He had to argue using all his exegetical skills that the Catholic Jesus did not complete the job of Messiah and explain why he had not. We will see how he uses his method to deal with these two obstacles to the spread of the unified Tetragram. First let us make clear this was his agenda. In *Sefer Edut* written not long after he was allowed into the Holy of Holies, he writes:

> And know that most of the visions that Raziel saw where all structured around the knowledge and renewed revelation of the Divine name (*shem ha meforash*) now in the world, in these days , it has not been like this since Adam till now, and it is the root of all his books … And he first wrote this in another book he wrote which he called *Get ha-shemot* and he intended to reveal to every man of intellect that the (Divine) names are the rulers in the world …But they are like nothing in comparison with the Kingship of the four lettered Hidden Name which is King of all Kings, and by it alone the Lord wishes to be known…therefore, Raziel denied kingship to all the other attributed names, and crown this name alone. (Hames, 2007, p. 85)

The focus on the Tetragram can be seen throughout his writings in some of which he still refuses to write the name out fully following Rabbinic systems of substitute such as יי or ה. His interpretation of Exodus 3 meant for him that it was the Tetragram that would be used to affect the redemption as in the day of Moses. "Who told from the first to the sons of Israel that they will be redeemed in the name of Yahuah?" (Abulafia, [2001]1288) Here Abulafia uses the *peshat* meaning but at the same time gives his own application to the text in that he was applying it to his own generation, placing him or King Messiah in the place of Moses. The next step then is to see how Abulafia equates the Father, Son and Holy Ghost of the Church with the *Adonai* of the Rabbis his understanding being that through his exegesis both needed to be replaced by Yahuah. Idel shows this. Abulafia connects the Trinity to *adonai* and the Father and the Son having the same weight by inserting the Trinity into the ten *sefirot* of Sefer Yetzirah by using the single letter method followed by gematria:

> The first letter of the Hebrew Alphabet points to the Holy Spirit according to Sefer Yetzirah, where the phrase *Sefirah Ahat* is understood by Abulafia as number one and when the second letter bet is added to the first letter the

word AV emerges namely Father, then when the letters from three to ten are added the figure 52 emerges that is *Ben* Son. Thus the idea is that within the ten *sefirot* namely the three first letters / numbers, the Trinity is found. This Trinity should be understood as a unity. And any separation between them is conceived of as being heretical. When the definite forms of the Father and the Son in the Hebrew characters are calculated Ha Av ha Ben [האב הבן] they amount to 65 which is the numerical value of the divine name Adonai [אדני] (Idel, 2007, p. 316)

This reading of the Father and the Son into the Holy Spirit into the *Sefirot* is very important and its association with *adonai* even more so. It combined with the note above regarding those who follow the way of the nations and brings equivalence in his treatment of the Rabbis with the treatment of doctrine of the nations (Christians included).

Finally we can take a short glance as to how Abulafia understood his relationship to the Jesus of the Catholic Church. First we find that even as he saw that he was fulfilling the prophecy of Moses to redeem Israel with the complete name of Yahuah so it was that he was *completing* the work of the Catholic Jesus. He indicates that he became master of Jesus of the Catholics but this mastery did not simply mean the destruction of the

Catholic Jesus but rather even as the Intellect exceeded but did not eliminate the imagination so Abulaifia felt he would exceed Jesus and bring what he symbolized, that which Abulafia learnt about that Jesus from the Rabbinic tradition and from Catholic tradition. The way he as Raziel seems to have dealt with Jesus is by imitating his ministry but on what he understood was a higher level. This meant somehow interpreting Christian revelation but as one who had a problem with Creation the *olam hazeh*, which was for him symbolized or came through Jesus and its imperfections were connected to the Catholic Jesus. Thus John 1:1 in commenting on Genesis 1:1 and perhaps the Wisdom tradition of Proverbs 8 says of the Word, Jesus "All things came into being through him, and without him not even one thing came into being that has not come into being" (Jn 1:2). For John this is a positive thing. But Abulafia in looking at the imperfect material creation notes regarding the character he called Jesus ben Pantera who was conceived during his mother's menstrual impurity "That blood is the mystery of primordial matter of which all created things are made and whereby they bear a common name" (Idel, 1988/2, p. 53). The other connection with creation is seen in Abulafia's reflection on the days of creation. Genesis 2:1-4 is seen in

Rabbinic tradition as indicating the creation of this age and the age to come. In the Talmud the small *heh* in Genesis 2:4 is seen as indicating that the text is mystically pointing to the creation of the present world in Abraham. However Abulafia takes this same text and argues that the present world is created using *yod heh* and the olam haba is created by vav heh. However for him yod heh represent Yeshua Ha notzri and *vav heh* represents King Messiah or Abulafia coming with the name Zecharyahu. Thus we see another parallel. Jesus is called a seal and King Messiah is called a seal. Jesus is the seal of the sixth day when the work was incomplete and King Messiah is the seal of the seventh day. Thus Abulafia has a very special position for Jesus in his system using *notaricon*. Third we will look at an illustration of Abulafia completing or imitating the work which Jesus begun. Rabbinic tradition knows little of an accursed Messiah hanging on a tree[89] for the sake of others. But Abulafia argues that Jesus was hung on the tree of knowledge of God and evil but the King Messiah was hanging on the tree of life on which everything

---

[89] Although early traditions in the Talmud like the NT read Isaiah 53 as the Messiah.

depends (Hames, 2007, p. 80). Finally Abulafia also wrote what he called half a book representing the first half of the name יהוה which Abulafia understood it was his or *melekh mashiach's* job to unite, thus Jesus Gospel represented יה that is Yah and in fact the 6th day and *melekh mashiach* would come in the power of הו. In addition the *melekh mashiach* will also come in the power of יה which means he will come with the complete power of the unified name and is therefore able to effect the complete redemption needed. Because Mashiach would come in the unified name יהוה he had the right to be called "God and the son of God". But because Jesus of Nazareth only came in the name יהseen in his name י-שוע ה-נוצרי he had no right to be called son of God, or God. We have at least two witnesses for this claim of Abulafia to being the son of God and as *melekh mashiach* the right to be called by the name יהוה (Hames, 2007, p. 80).

Conclusion

Thus we have seen that Abulafia's is definitely no Rashbam not even a Rashi, rather he part of the stream which flowed through Maimonides and Nachmanides. Abulafis place in the Medieval exegesis had to be as unifier of all methods both Jews and Gentile through his unique call as a prophet.

Appendix 1: The Books

	ספר היי העולם הבא	
A Secret of Blowing the Shofar	סוד תקיעת שופר מ1	
	ספר צרוף שם המיוחד מטטרון מ1	
Book of Witness	ספר עדות מ3	
-Hidden Treasure of Eden	אוצר עדן גנוז מ1	
Furnace of the mind	מצרף השכל	

The Walled Garden	ספר גן נעול 4מ	
Light of the Intellect	אור השכל 31מ	
Secrets of the Torah	סתרי תורה 42מ	
Seven Paths of the Torah	אגרת שבע נתיבות התורה 10מ	
A book of the Man Adam	ספר איש אדם 3מ	
The Letter	ספר האות [חזיון זכריה]10מ	
Words of Beauty	אמרי שפר 19מ	
The New Covenant	ספר הברית החדשה 2מ	
Book of Redemption	ספר גאולה 2מ	
The Divorce	ספר הגט 2מ	

The Haftorah	ספר ההפטרה 4מ	
And this to Yehudah	אגרת וזאת ליהודה 17	
Seal of the Haftorah	חותם הפטרה 2מ	
Life of the Soul	חיי הנפש 76מ	
The Life	ספר החיים 3מ	
The Desire	ספר החשק 1	
The Book of the Upright	ספר הישר 9	
The Recommended Book	ספר המליץ 3מ	
The Teaching	ספר המלמד 1מ	
Key of the Sefirot	מפתח הספירות 1	Numbers
The key of	מפתח התכחות	Deuteronomy

sanctions	מ1	
Key of names	מפתח השמות	Exodus
Key to sacrifices	מפתח קורבנות	leviticus
	אוצר עדן גנוז	
The key of wisdom	מפתח החכמות	genesis
Keys	ספר המפתחות מ4	
Melting Pot to silver	מצרף לכסף מ3	
Secret of Jerusalem	סוד ירושלים מ3	
Secret to Activating the Name	סוד פעולה השם מ3	
He sent the Hand of creation attain	פיוט :שלח יד ברואה להשיג מ1	
To the blood redeemer I	פיוט :אל מגואלי דם אצעק מ1	

screamed		
Nine Fires in Ancient Parable	פיוט: "אשתשע במשל קדמין 14מ	
Interpreattion about the Torah	פרושים על התורה 1מ	
Refining	ספר הצרוף 4מ	
Guardian of the Commandment	שומר מצוה 2מ	
Praise of the Creation	תהילה היצרה 8מ	
Sanctuary of the mind	משכן השכל	

Appendix 2: Synopses of Lahy Edition

The Sign is divided into eleven chapters, each chapter is split into paragraphs which we will call verses. The chapters have the following verses: 1-24,2-18[90],3-3, 4-36, 5-58, 6-14,7-22,8-8,9-17, 10-15, 11-73. Thus we have a book of approximately 288 verses[91]. In terms of Lahy's edition the three sections of Hames analysis begin at chapter 1 verse 1 "in the seventh year of the reign of Messiah", chapter 5 verse 54 "In the year 5045" and chapter 11 verse 1 "on the fourth day of the seventh month, which corresponds to the first moon of the start of

---

[90] In verse 15 of the second chapter the Lahy and the Gros editions have a difference in the text. In the Lahy printed edition the text begins with tav as in tet vav, the mark or sign, as in Ezekiel 9 representing a cross in some tradition however at this point the Gros edition has the word tet gimel. The Lahy edition reads תו צכאי עקר whereas the Gros edition reads תג צבאי עקר .

[91] The division of the Amnon Gros edition has a different chapter division. It also has 11 chapters with the following numbers 1-24, 2-18, 3-3, 4-93, 5-7, 6-14, 7-23, 8-8, 9-17, 10-18, 11-80. This gives a total number of verses of 305. However some of this is due to different verse divisions which we can not look at here. For example chapter 4 verse 9 of Lahy is two verses in Gros. We also find another different with Lahy having a caph and the beginning of verse 10 where Gros has a beth. Since Lahy does translation at least we know their words make sense.

the eighteenth year of my visions" (Hames, 2006, p. 182). Hames dates the first section to late 1283, based on the revelation of December 12, 1276 mentioned above, plus seven years, the second section to 10th November 1284, and the third section to *tishrei* 1288. However in view of Abulafia's dating the Sign from 1270-71 and in another comment he indicates that the Messiah in 1288 had been Messiah for 18years We see then two parts were written during the 15 years of torment and the third after his soul had come to rest and after he had been in Comino for almost three years. It is that second section from chapter 5:54 to chapter 10:15 of Lahy that is the completion of *Habsorah*, as can be seen below the word gospel occurs in it a number of times.

The first chapter has 24 paragraphs and is an acrostic text following the order of the alphabet with Aleph to Tav and then Aleph to Beth[92]. Verses 1 to 7 are testimonies in the first person. Paragraphs 8 to 14 describe the author's battles with the enemy,

---

[92] He uses the form seen for samekh.

and 15 to 22 encourage the people of Yahuah to rejoice in what Yahuah is doing. Verse 22 talks of the letter Tav as a sign. Since the accepted shape of a tav in some circles is a cross, this might for a disciples hint at the gospel. Chapter 2 has 20 verses, verses 1-8 give prophetic words in the name of Yahuah Elohei Israel. Verses 9-14 give the 72, 3 letter names of the Shem hameforash based on Exodus 14:19-21. These names can also be seen as 54 four letter names (Lahy, 2007, p. 23n.17). Verses 15 to 20 begin again with the *tav*[93] and there seems to be imagery of a battle in relation to the limbs of the body in line with way 4 of seven ways above. Verse 19 plays on the word *gad* and mentions H-U. Verse 20 finishes with the words li yeshuatcem qavinu yahadonahi. This last word is a *shem beshem* with the name adonai inside the name Yahuah. Chapter three has three verses which contain the divine name only once. Here he focuses on the day of judgment and the Holy Spirit, which is central to the gospel message and Yahuah is

––––––––––––––––––––

[93] In Gros with tag

presented as God of Judgement" (Abulafia, [2001]1288, p. 129). An interesting phrase which might remind one of the Nicene creed which states that the son is "light from light" is the phrase "Light from his light" ('or me'or) . Chapter four has 36 verses and is by far the most mystical of the chapters. It brings a lot of renditions of the *Shem hameforash* based on Exodus 14:19-21 where there are three verses in the biblical text each with seventy two letters. The first time in *The Sign*, Abulafia gives the 216 letter name is in chapter two. He introduces it " הנה השם הגדול והנורה מרבע ומשלש חקוק כאשר הראני יהוה" Behold the great and terrible name square and triangle, engraved as Yahuah showed me". As a triangle it had three letters and as a square four letters, thus 72 names or 54 names (Lahy, 2007, p. 23n.18) We know from the seventh method that this name was used to enable the practitioner to attain prophecy. Indeed one of Abulafia's disciples in sharing his terrifying experience having meditated using the name was told "and who was it who allowed you to touch the Name? Did I not tell you to permute only letters" (Disciple A, 1976). The testimony of the disciples gives us clearer understanding of how disciples might end up taking baptism after listening to Abulafia. The forces they deal with when following his method are beyond their capacity to control. The disciple testifies that Abulafia told him he had reached a high degree of prophecy but wanted to free him from it because he had seen that his face had changed. In the same way he tries to explain away parallels between his Trinity and the Christian Trinity, in both cases he was not entirely successful. The disciple protested 'In heavens name, can you perhaps impart to me some power to enable me to bear this force emerging from my heart and to receive influx from it?" Abulafia answered him "My son, it is the Lord who must bestow such power upon you for such power is not within man's control" (Disciple A, 1976, p. 141). Thus Abulafia was leading his disciples out into the ocean and from there they needed to sink or swim. His teaching took them beyond the bounds of religious tradition to spiritual encounters which they could not control. Regarding the seventy two names which Abulafia lists in different ways in *The Sign*, even transforming through the substitution method of *atbash* in chapter 4 verse 15. The disciple says "I set out to take the Great Name of God, consisting of seventy two names, permuting and combining it. But when I had done this for a little while, behold the letters took on in my eyes the shape of great mountains, strong, trembling seized me and I could summon no strength, my hair stood on end, and it was as if I was not in this world" (Disciple A, 1976, p. 141). Even this reminds us of the words of the Apostle Paul "I knew a man in Messiah above fourteen years ago (whether in the body, I cannot tell; or whether out of the body, I cannot tell: God knoweth) such a one caught up to the third heaven. And I knew such a man, (whether in the body, or out of the body I cannot tell: God knoweth;) How that he was caught up into paradise, and heard unspeakable words, which it is not lawful for man to utter"(2 Cor 12). In some sense the experience of Abulafia's disciple would seem to be the opposite for his goes on to say "and behold something resembling speech emerged from my heart and came to my lips and forced them to move. I thought – perhaps this is a spirit of madness that has entered into me? But behold, I saw it uttering wisdom. I said "This is indeed the spirit of wisdom" (Disciple A, 1976, p. 141). This experiences of his mouth being taken over and him beginning to speak words reminds us of the birth of the Church on Pentecost. Where the Holy Spirit fell on them "And they began to speak in other tongues as the Spirit gave them utterance"(Acts 2:4). Both the disciples of Abulafia began to speak words from a source which they did not control. Of course these experiential parallels would not be enough to cause a man to take baptism, but combined with reflection of the similarities between the teachings it might do. Indeed first the foundation of the Rabbinic Jewish antipathy to Yeshu would have to be shaken and then a possible alternative path might be considered. The dangers of this can be seen again in the words of the disciple. During his studies he discovered a temptation to leave Torah and Talmud behind "And God is my witness: if I had not previously acquired strength of faith by what little I had learned of the Torah and the Talmud, the impulse to keep many of the religious commands would have left me, although the fire of pure intention was ablaze in my heart" (Disciple A, 1976, p. 139). This temptation to leave did not come from Abulafia but from his previous studies of *the Guide to the Perplexed*, the very thing we noted earlier the Kabbalists and Abner of Borgas protested against. This shows us that some of the disciples of Abulafia through their studies of Philosophy may already have been on the verge of leaving Judaism and his ideas may have just strengthened their decision to make such a daring and difficult move.

Chapter 5 of the Sign includes meditation on Yod heh vav heh. In this chapter Abulafia focuses more on his role as Zechariah one who remembers the name Yahuah. What is interesting is how he describes himself as a *mevaser* proclaiming a *basorah*. These are favorite NT terms and the *mevaser* would be translated evangelist in the NT. Paul quotes Isaiah 52:7 in this respect, and Abulafia uses this terminology of himself in chapter 5:11, and 14. In this chapter he like the Apostle Paul before him and Jeremiah and Jonah before him is commanded to speak to the Gentiles "and they believed in the good news of Yahuah'. In chapter 6 the focus is still on Zechariah. His name being connected with remembering the name of Yahuah.

In chapter 7 he mentions his mission to Comtina having moved from city to city and place to place he finally settles in the small Island where according to chapter 7 verse 3 Yahuah commanded him to write the book. Chapter 8-10 are similar but in chapter 11 he really enters into an apocalyptic vision. According Hames this is the section from which the name of the book comes. He dates it very carefully, if inaccurately, and sees a man on a horse coming with 22000 men from the West, He has a sign on his forehead. The whole vision reminds us of Daniel and Revelation. We are not given clarity as to the meaning of the Sign, but the point we can make is this was a vision which he did not control. According to Idel and Elior, Abulafia had had visions of Jesus Christ which he may have perceived as demonic attacked and had repelled them, but of course if he taught his disciples how to receive visions they too could have such visions, but it is possible they would accept them, and hence be baptized.

Appendix 3

The fruit of the ministry of this prophet is seen in the history of Judaism among disciples of baal shem tov and his chasidim, through Rabbi Shneur Zalman and his Tanya and the Chabad of the recent deceased messiah designate, Rabbi Menachem Mendel Sneerson and the expected Yehoshua of Rabbi Yitzhak Kaduri (Nachman, 2012). In the history of Christianity in the many Jews who turned to Jesus of Nazareth in 1295 after the redemption sign seen in the form of crosses appearing all over the garments of the Jewish community waiting for the sign of Messianic redemption (Baer, 1961), the mass "conversions" (forced and voluntary) of Jews in the late 13th century in Spain and in southern Italy (Hames, 2000). The conversion of Rabbi Avner of Burgos, the most famous Jewish "convert"[94] in medieval history who became author of many Hebrew books and "It was Abner who fathered that ideology of apostasy which was destined about two generations after his death, to bring wrack and ruin upon Spanish Jewry" (Baer, 1961, p. 330) . As in the case of Jeremiah the prophet, and Jesus of Nazareth who were both

---

[94] In Jewish eyes infamous apostate

prophets who were rejected before Abulafia, the rejection of Abulafia by his home country Spain was followed by mixed results. Jeremiah and Jesus (through his disciples) like Abulafia prophesied both to Jews and Gentiles. Their messages to their brethren the Jews were in the main rejected. Thus the rejection of Jeremiah lead to the destruction of Jerusalem and the exile in Babylon. Jeremiah began prophesying in about 627-626 BC and Jerusalem was burnt 587-586 BC (Scofield, 1917). Jesus began his ministry around 27/28 AD and Rabbinic tradition holds that the temple was destroyed around 68AD (Hames, 2007, p. 76) [95]. Regarding Jesus a number of streams of Rabbinic thought circulated around him after his rejection. Many of these can be seen represented in the work of Morton Smith, Jesus the Magician, where he looks at the opinions of "outsiders" on Jesus of Nazareth. The

---

[95] Although in the Rabbinic tradition regarding the three ages of history, 2000 years of Chaos, 2000 years of Torah from Abraham and 2000 years of Messiah, the 2000 years of Messiah began in 172 AD. The difference from the calculation of Ussher being 240 years, that is 68 + 172 = 240. In the Talmud the Rabbi's dated from the destruction of the Temple. In the school of Elijah the three ages are as outline here. The Messianic age begin followed by Shabbat the seventh day. History then is 7000 years and a day is a year. (Tractate Sanhedrin 96B

Rabbinic Jewish position on him can be seen in the *Dialogue with Trypho* between Justin Martyr and Rabbi Trypho (mid 2nd C.) and Origin against Celsus (3rd C.) where Celsus taps into some Rabbinic Jewish traditions regarding Jesus. Some of these traditions found their way into *Toldot Yeshu*[96], a Rabbinic parody or satire of the gospels. Jesus is no longer son of God through Virgin Mary but son of Joseph Pantera a roman soldier who seduces the innocent Jewish girl Mary. However he remains a worker of wondrous signs but as was Smith's thesis he was a sorcerer (*goes*) not a prophet for those outsiders (Smith, 1970). In *Toldot Yeshu*, the character representing Jesus, called Yeshu is a disciple of Rabbi Yehoshua ben Paraciah one of the zugot of Rabbinic sages in the Pirkei Avot and lived in the period about 80 BC. This character is repulsed by Yehoshua ben Parachiah because of a sin and goes astray. He obtains miraculous powers by gaining access to the Tetragrammaton. He went into the temple, where the name was written, wrote it down, cut his skin and placed the name into his skin. As he left the temple the

---

[96] Hugh Schonfield argued that Toldot Yeshu was a reflection on the Gospel of the Hebrews mentioned in the writings of the Church Fathers.

dogs their barked at him as they did to everyone and he forget the name. However when he left he retrieved the name by taking the parchment out of his skin. He then saying *yod heh vav heh* and performing miracle using the letters of the name. This tradition was circulated in the Middle Ages and was Abulafia's Jesus was the son of Pantera. At the same time Rabbinic tradition applied Notaricon and Gematria to the name of Jesus. The name of Jesus Yahushua (397), Yahusha (391) or Yeshua (386)[97] was changed to yesh"u יש"ו. By the exegetical method of *notaricon*, where the name become an acronym, the three letters were read as ימחה[98] ש-מו ו-

_____

[97] This has the same number as the word tongue which was the whole basis of Abulafia's system. It was through the tongue man gained entrance into the world to come.
[98] The word imchah coming from the root mem chet heh can mean wipe out, blot out a name and strike or hit. It is used in the exact form yod mem chat heh as a jussive in three verses Deu 25:6, Jud 21:17, 2 Kg 21:13. But the most interesting reference may be Deu 29:18-20 where all the curses of the Torah are said to come on a man who secretly goes to worship strange gods.

Deu 29:19 (29:18) והיה בשמעו את־דברי האלה הזאת
והתברך בלבבו לאמר שלום יהיה־לי כי בשררות
לבי אלך למען ספות הרוה את־הצמאה:
Deu 29:20 (29:19) לא־יאבה יהוה סלח לו כי אז יעשן
אף־יהוה וקנאתו באיש ההוא ורבצה בו כל־האלה

זכרו.This rereading of Jesus name meant his number was npw

Appendix 4 Abulafia as high priest and prophet of the pen

As a prophet of the pen Abulafia uses a number of paths in understanding the Torah or rather as keys[99] to the Scripture which enable one to unite with YHWH (yod heh vav heh) in what Abulafia calls the Holy of Holies[100]. This temple imagery is very important for Abulafia. He saw the pen as a tool of temple service as a high priest in the Holy of Holies. He lived in this world but also in the world of vision. Wolfson makes a very important point about the liturgical importance of Abulafia's pen:

"That Abulafia conceived of meditation of liturgical worship is... explicit (Wolfson, 2000, p. 209). This

---

הכתובה בספר הזה ומחה יהוה את־שמו מתחת
השמים:

This is interesting because the early preached regarding the name of Yahushua "There is no other name under heaven given among men whereby we may be saved" (Acts and this verse in

[99] Each of his five commentaries on the five book of Moses is called a *mafteach* or key

[100] The place from which prophesy issues forth.

meditation consisted of permutating names of God with pen and ink. Abulafia prepares his students to enter the temple, even the Holy of Holies very carefully "Prepare yourself to unify your heart and purify your body, and select a special place where your voice will not be heard by any person, and you will be alone so that you may meditate without another.[101]...And wrap yourself in your prayer shawl and place phylacteries [tefillin] on your head and your arm if you can so that you will not fear and tremble on account of the Shekinah who is with you at that time"[102]. In Rabbinic tradition the

---

[101] We can compare these words of Jesus who Abulafia claims to be succeeding in the role of the use of the name of Yahuah (yod heh vav heh), Jesus represented the first two letters of the Tetragram yod heh where as Melekh mashiach come with the power of the second two letters vav heh but as the role of unifying these two with yod heh and the in unifying the name he has the right to be called God and son of God which Jesus did not have because he only came with half the name. In respect to prayer (Meditation) Jesus said : Mat 6:6 But thou, when thou prayest, enter into thy closet, and when thou hast shut thy door, pray to thy Father which is in secret; and thy Father which seeth in secret shall reward thee openly. We will find that getting your prayers answered is a key element of Abulafia's holy of holies for the man who has the right to be called by the name Yahuah.

[102] (Wolfson, 2000, p. 209)

123

Skekinah was Yahuah's presence in the Holy of Holies. Abulafia then as removed the need for a physical geographical location for the issuing of Mosaic level prophecy from the holy of holies. In addition the requirement for no one to hear him could be based on the rabbinic prohibition on speaking the name Yahuah which prohibition Abulafia has been sent to overturn and of course the exegetical reasoning which went with it. Abulafia makes this clear in many places but clearly in the second section of the Sign:

> On the same day, Zecharyahu the shepherd
> will begin to write miracles of wisdom
> and wise thoughts by means of the letters of the Torah.
> From these letters Zecharyahu will explain the distinct name
> and will expand the Tetragrammaton
> and will unify the' special name [of God].
> He will place it [his name] in the mouth of his disciples and teach it to
> those who follow him until he reveals his secrets and has made
> known his end times. He teaches his ways to all those of a wise
> So that it can again be pronounced without fear.

Thus in *the Sign*, in the second section there is a character whose name is Zecharyahu which means he remembers the name. This character is a shepherd for Yahuah peoples and his job is manifold but a key function is to unify the name of Yahuah and to place it in the mouth of his disciples. All the scholars point out that the way Abulafia spells the name Zecharyahu with a vav on the end זכריהו gives it the same number as circumcised Abraham אברהם.[103] This of course is Abulafia's first name. Thus using the Gematria system the two names weigh the same in terms of *the creators method in sefer Yetzirah every word* with the same number values as a building block of creation weight the same.

Bibliography

Abulafia, 1240-1291. *Hayye ha-Olam ha-Ba.* s.l.:s.n.

103

Abulafia, A., [2001]1288. ספר האות. In: מצרף השכל וספר
האות. ירושלים: s.n.

Abulafia, A., 1271-1290. *Shomer Mitzvah.* s.l.:s.n.

Abulafia, A., 1887. *We Zot li- Yihudah.* s.l.:s.n.

Abulafia, A., 1943 [1286ff]. Every Man His Own Messiah.
In: L. Scwartz, ed. *Memoirs of my People Through a
Thousand Years.* Philadelphia: The Jewisgh Publication
Society of America, pp. 21-29.

Abulafia, A., 1976. The Question of Prophecy. In: *The
Secret Garden.* New York: The Seabury Press, pp. 117-
136.

Abulafia, A., 2001. *Sefer Geula.* s.l.:s.n.

Abulafia, A., 2007. *Le Livre du Signe.* Roquevaire :
Editions Lahy.

Abulafia, M., pre 1285. *Mafteach ha-Hokhmot.* s.l.:s.n.

Abulafia, M., pre 1285. *Matzref la-Ketsef.* s.l.:s.n.

Abulafia, O., pre 1285. *Otzar Eden Ganuz.* s.l.:s.n.

Abulafia, W., 1270-1285. *Seven Ways of the Torah.*
s.l.:s.n.

Baer, Y., 1940. 'Hareka 'Hahistori shelRaya Mehemna. Volume 5, pp. 1-44.

Baer, Y., 1961. *A History of the Jews in Christian Spain.* s.l.:The Jewish Publication Society of America.

Bernfeld, S., 1931. *בני עליה.* Tel Aviv: s.n.

Besserman, P., 2006. *A New Kabbalah For Women.* New York: Palgrave Macmillan .

Bloom, H., 2002. Foreword. In: *Absorbing Perfections, Kaballah and Interpretation.* New Haven: Yale University Press, pp. ix-xiv.

Bokser, B. Z., 1993 [1981]. *The Jewish Mystical Tradition.* London: Jason Aronson Inc..

Caroll, R., 1993. *Jeremiah.* Sheffield: JSOT Press.

Crone, P., n.d. Hagarism. In: s.l.:s.n.

Dan, J., 2002. *The Heart and the Fountain: An anthology of Jewish Mystical Experiences.* Oxford: Oxford University Press.

Disciple A, A., 1976. Shaarei Tzedek. In: *The Secret Garden.* New York: The seabury Press, pp. 137-145.

Drazin, I., 2014. *Mysteries of Judaism.* Jerusalem: Gefen.

127

Durant, W., 1950. *The Story of Civilisation: The Age of Faith.* s.l.:s.n.

Emden, J., 1757. *Seder Olam Rabba veZuta.* s.l.:s.n.

Emden, J., 1757. *Seder Olam Rabbah ve Zuta" The Order of the World Great and Small.* Hamburg: s.n.

Falk, H., 1982. Rabbi Jacob Emden's Views on Christianity. *Journal of Ecumenical Studies,* 19(1).

Faulstich, E., 1990. *Bible Chronlogy and the Scientific Method.* s.l.:The Bible Chronologist.

Friedlander, M., 1877. *Essays on the writings of Abraham Ibn Ezra.* London: s.n.

Garber, Z., ed., 2011. The Kabbalah of Rabbi Jesus. In: *The Jewish Jesus: Revelation, Reflection, Reclamation.* West Lafayette: Purdue University Press, pp. 20-35.

Goldin, S., 2014. *Apostasy and Jewish Identity in High Middle Ages Northern Europe.* Manchester: Manchester University Press.

Gottheil, A., 1906. Avraham of Avila. In: *Jewish Encylopedia.* s.l.:s.n.

Graetz, H., 1894. *History of the Jews Vol IV.*
Philadelphai: The Jewish Publication Society of America.

Graetz, H., 1956. *History of the Jews.* Phildelphia: The
Jeiwsh Publication society.

Greenstein, E., 2005. Medieval Bible Commentaries. In:
Back to the Sources. New York: Summit Books.

Hames, H., 2000. *The Art of Conversion: Christianity and
Kabbalah in the 13th Century.* Leiden: s.n.

Hames, H., 2005. "From Calabria comeith the Law, and
the Word of the Lord from Sicily : The Holy Land in the
Thought of Joachim of Fiore and Abraham Abulafia.
Mediteranean Historical Review 20,, 20(2), pp. 187-199.

Hames, H., 2005. *From Calbria Cometh the Law, and the
Word of the Lord from Sicily: The Holy Land in the
Thought of Joachim of Fiore and Abraham Abulafia.*
s.l.:Taylor and Francis.

Hames, H., 2006. Three in One or One that is Three: On
the Dating of Abraham Abulafia's Sefer Ha OT. *Revue
des Etudes Juives,* Volume 165, pp. 179-190.

Hames, H., 2007. *Like Angels on Jacobs Ladder.* New
York: State Univerrsity of New York Press.

Hofer, N., 2013. Abraham Abulafia's "Mystical" reading of the Gudie for the Perplexed. *Numen: International review for the History of Religions,* 60(2/3), pp. 251-279.

Hylton, A., 2013. Reflections on the Use of the Name Yahuwah (Yahweh) or IAO in the Early Church. *International Journal of Humanities and Social Science ,* 3(4 Speical Edition), pp. 91-97.

Idel, M, 1998. Abulafia's Secrets of the Guide: A linguistic Turn. In: *Perspec tives on Jewish Thought and Mysticism.* s.l.:s.n., pp. 289-329.

Idel, M., 1936 . *kitvei r abraham abulafia vemishnato.* Jerusalem: Hebrew University.

Idel, M., 1976. *Abulafia, His Works and Doctines: Doctoral Thesis [Hebrew].* Jerusalem: Hebrew University.

Idel, M., 1988/2. *Studies in Ecstatic Kabbalah.* New York: New York state University.

Idel, M., 1988. *Kabbalah in New Perspectives.* New Haven and London: Yale University Press.

Idel, M., 1988. *The Mystical Experience in Abulafia.* New York: Albany.

Idel, M., 1989. *Language, Torah, and Hermeneutics in Abraham Abulafia.* New York: State University of New York.

Idel, M., 1993. Introduction to the Bison Book Edition. In: *On the Art of the Kabbalah.* s.l.:University of Nebraska Press, pp. v - xxix.

Idel, M., 2002. *Absorbing Perfections.* New Haven: Yale University Press.

Idel, M., 2002. *Absorbing Perfections.* New Haven: Yale Universty Press.

Idel, M., 2007, 2015.. "Abulafia, Abraham ben Samuel." Detroit: , 2007. 337-339.. *Encyclopaedia Judaica.,* 23 April, Volume 2nd ed. Vol. 1. , pp. 337-339.

Idel, M., 2007. *Ben: Sonship and Jewish Mysticism.* London: Continuum.

Idel, M., 2012. A Kabbalist "Son of God" on Jesus and Christianity. In: *Jesus Among the Jews: Representation and Thought.* Abingdon: Routledge, pp. 61-93.

JE, 1906. *Abraham Abulafia.* s.l.:s.n.

Jellinek, A., 1853. *גנזי חכמת הקבלה*Auswahl *kabbalistischer Mystik.* Leipzig: s.n.

Jellinek, A., 1854. *Philosophie und Kabbala, Erstes Heft, enthaelt Abraham Abulafia's Sendschreiben ueber Philosophie und Kabbala.* Leipzig: s.n.

Jellinek, A., 1887. Preface. In: Jellinek, ed. *Sefer Ha Ot.* s.l.:s.n.

Jellinek, A., 1887. Sefer Ha Oth, Apocalypse des Pseudo-Propheten und Pseudo-Messias Abraham Abulafia. *Jubelschrift zum siebzigsten Geburstage des H. Graetz,* pp. 65-88.

Kamin, S., 1985. *Affinities Between Jewqish and Christian Exegesis in Twelfth Century Northern France.* Jerusalem, The Magnes Press.

Kamin, S., 1986. *Rashi's Exegetical Categorization in Respect to the Distinction Between Peshat and Derash.* Jerusalem: s.n.

Kaufmann, K. & et.al, 1906. Abraham Abulafia. In: *Jewish Encyclopedia.* s.l.:s.n.

Lahy, G., 2007. *Le Livre du Signe, Sefer Ha Oth.* Roquevaire: s.n.

Landauer, M., 1845. Vorslaefigur Bericht in Ansehung des Sohar. *Megen Blatt.*

Lerner, R., 2001. *The Feast of Saint Abraham.*
Philadelphia: University of Pennsylvania.

Liebes, Y., 1993. *Studies in the Zohar.* New York: State
University of New York.

Macgregor Mathers, S., 1888. *Kabbalah Denudata
:Kabbalah Unveiled.* s.l.:Black mask online.

Maimonides, 1135-1204. Hilcot Melakim.

Maimonides, 1135-1204. Of Prophecy. In: L. Schwartz,
ed. *A Golden Treasury of Jewish Literature.* London:
Arthur Baker Ltd, pp. 686-690.

Maimonides, M., 1135-1204. *The Eight Chapters.*
London: Modechai Institute.

Margolis, M. & Marx, A., 1947. *A Hisotry of the Jewish
People.* Philadelphia: The Jewish Publication Society of
America.

Mendes-Flohr, P., 1994. Introductory Essay: The
Spiritual Quest of the Philologist. In: *Gershom Scholem
The Man and His Work.* New York: State University of
New York press, pp. 1-29.

Mowinckel, S., 2002. *The Spirit and the Word.* s.l.:s.n.

Nachman, M., 2012. *The King is Here.* s.l.:Iuniverse.

Nachman, M., 2013. Mi Avihem. *International Journal of Advanced Research,* 1(8), pp. 652-666.

Petersen, D., 1981. *The Role of Israel's Prophets.* Sheffield: Fortress Press.

Rabow, J., 2003. *50 Jewish Messiahs.* Jerusalem: Gefen Publishing House.

Reuchlin, J., 1983. *On the Art of the Kabbalah.* Nabraska: University of Nabraska.

Rosentreich, N., 1977/8. Symbolism and Transcendence: On SA sedme Philosophical of Gersom Scholem's Opus.. *Revue of Metaphysics,* Volume 31, p. 605.

Scholem, G., 1954. *Major Trends in Jewish Mysticism.* New York: Schocken Books.

Scholem, G., 1971. Abraham Abulafia. In: *Encyclopedia Judaica.* s.l.:Keter Publishing.

Scholem, G., 1974. *Kabbalah.* Jerusalem: Keter.

Schonfield, H., 1984. *The Essene Odyssey, The mystery of the True Teacher & Essene Impact on the Shaping of Human Destiny.* Shaftesbury: Element Books.

Schonfield, H., 1993. *The Essene Odyssey.* s.l.:Element
Books.

Scofield, C., 1917. *The Scofield Refernce Bible.* Oxford:
Oxford University Press.

Smith, M., 1970. *Jesus the Magician.* s.l.:s.n.

Wirszubski, C., 1989. *Pico Della Mirandol's Encounter
With Jewish Mysticism.* Jerusalem: The Israel Academy
of Sciences and Humanites.

Wolfson, E., 2000. *Abraham Abulafia- Kabbalist and
Prophet Hermeneutic, Theosophy, and Theurgy.* Los
Angeles: Cherub Press.

Zechariah, A., 1976. The Book of the Letter. In: *The
Secret Garden.* New York: The seabury Press, pp. 124-
135.

אבולעפיא, א., 1285ff. *שבע נתיבות התורה.* s.l.:s.n.

CPSIA information can be obtained
at www.ICGtesting.com
Printed in the USA
BVHW071703090620
581035BV00002B/160

9 781365 373343